The Autobiography of
ST. IGNATIUS LOYOLA
WITH RELATED DOCUMENTS

Translated by
JOSEPH F. O'CALLAGHAN

Edited with Introduction and Notes by
JOHN C. OLIN

FORDHAM UNIVERSITY PRESS
New York

Copyright © 1992 by Fordham University Press
All rights reserved
LC 92–32959
ISBN 0–8232–1480–X
First published by Harper & Row, 1974
Fordham University Press, 1992

Fourth Printing, 1998

Library of Congress Cataloging-in-Publication Data

Ignatius, of Loyola, Saint, 1491–1556.
[Autobiografía. English]
The autobiography of St. Ignatius of Loyola, with related
documents / edited with introduction and notes by John C. Olin;
translated by Joseph F. O'Callaghan.
p.   cm.
Originally published: New York : Harper & Row, 1974.
Includes bibliographical references.
ISBN 0–8232–1480–X
1. Ignatius, of Loyola, Saint, 1491–1556.   2. Christian saints —
Spain — Biography.   I. Olin, John C.   II. O'Callaghan, Joseph F.
III. Title.
BX4700.L7A3413   1992
271'.5302 — dc20
[B]   92–32959
CIP

Printed in the United States of America

Contents

v

Illustrations

The illustrations are from the anonymous Vita beati P. Ignatii Loiolae *published in Rome in 1609, the year of Ignatius's beatification. This work, consisting of eighty engravings of scenes from the life of the saint, is attributed to Cornelis Galle the elder, one of a family of famous engravers of Antwerp. Several of the designs, including that for number 7 below, are said to have been done by Rubens. The reproductions here were made through the courtesy of the Woodstock College Library.*

*Sapientiam sanctorum narrent populi
et laudes eorum nuntiet
ecclesia.*

Introduction

Toward the end of his life St. Ignatius Loyola related the story of his earlier years—his pilgrim years—to an associate in Rome. This was done after long hesitation at the instance of several of his companions in the Society of Jesus who wanted him to tell how God had directed him and formed him since the time of his conversion. The account was to be, in the words of one of these companions, "a testament and paternal instruction" to his sons in the new religious order.[1] Ignatius's story thus was essentially an interior history, a history of inward transformation and spiritual growth, and its basic purpose was one of religious enlightenment and guidance. That does not mean, however, that Ignatius gave posterity simply a devotional tract or a revelation of purely spiritual dimensions. He had lived and traveled, studied and taught in a tumultuous world, and his religious experience, as profound or even as mystical as it was, occurred in the context of history. He was aware of this, and he related the story of his most formative years with as lively a sense of actual circumstance

1. From the preface to the autobiography by Jerome Nadal (1507–80), one of Ignatius's most trusted assistants and one of the most important members of the early Society of Jesus. *Fontes Narrativi de S. Ignatio de Loyola*, 4 vols. (Rome, 1943–65), I, 357. These volumes contain the basic sources and earliest *vitae* of St. Ignatius Loyola and are a part of the voluminous *Monumenta Historica Societatis Jesu*, 100 vols. (Madrid-Rome, 1894–1969). They will be referred to as *FN*.

as of divine direction. The *contemplatio in actione* that is said to charac-
terize his mature spirituality finds also its expression, and perhaps its
source, in his innate realism, that is, in his openness to life and in
his day-by-day involvement in it. For this reason Ignatius's autobiography is personal history in the richest sense of the word. It is
authentic, it is graphic, it has depth, it marvelously conveys the sense
of movement and development. "Every word," writes Pedro
Leturia, one of the great modern students of Ignatius, "contains a
fact or opens up a wide perspective."[2]

The autobiography was written under unusual circumstances.
Pressed by his colleagues, especially Jerome Nadal, Ignatius at
length agreed to recount the events of his early years to a young
Portuguese Jesuit then resident at the *casa professa* in Rome. This was
Luis Gonçalves da Câmara, who in his brief preface to the *Life* has
told us something of the circumstances of its being undertaken and
of the manner in which it was dictated and then later written down.
Ignatius began to tell his story to Câmara in September 1553, but
he soon interrupted his narration pleading illness or some important
business that required his attention. Nadal and Câmara, however,
finally persuaded him to resume his account, and he did so in March
1555; but he broke it off again in a very short time because of the
death of Pope Julius III, and it was not until late September that he
went back to it and brought it to completion. It was told thus to
Câmara in three relatively short installments. The latter listened
attentively and then immediately after his sessions with Ignatius
made notes. Later he filled out the story and dictated the text we
have to a scribe. The language is Spanish save for the last part of the
text which is in Italian because Câmara, finishing it in Genoa at the
end of 1555 as he traveled back to Portugal, did not have a Spanish-
speaking scribe available. It is generally conceded that Câmara had
an excellent memory (Nadal affirms it), and he himself declares in
his preface that he endeavored not to write a word he had not heard
from the mouth of Ignatius.

2. Pedro Leturia, S.J., *Iñigo de Loyola,* trans. Aloysius J. Owen, S.J. (Syracuse, 1949),
p. xi.

We do not have the original manuscript dictated by Câmara to his scribes, but there are several very old copies of the text, on the basis of which two critical editions have been published in the *Monumenta Historica Societatis Jesu,* the first in 1904 in the first volume of the *Scripta de Sancto Ignatio* and the second in 1943 in the first volume of the *Fontes Narrativi de S. Ignatio de Loyola.*[3] It is from the Spanish and Italian text in the *Fontes Narrativi* that our translation has been made. It is interesting to note that the original text was not printed until 1904, when it first appeared in the Jesuit *Monumenta,* although the Bollandists had published a very early Latin version by Father Annibal du Coudray in their *Acta Sanctorum* in 1731. The first vernacular versions to be published, it would seem, were two English translations from du Coudray's Latin text, both appearing in 1900. One was by E. M. Rix and was published in London with a very interesting introduction by George Tyrrell (who was then a Jesuit but later became a leading figure in the so-called Modernist movement) and an excellent bibliographical appendix by Herbert Thurston, S.J. The other was by J. F. X. O'Conor, S.J., and was published in New York. In 1956 a third English translation appeared, that of William J. Young, S.J., though it was actually the first to be made from the original Spanish and Italian text.[4] Our version, then, is the fourth English edition and is prompted by the need to have this important work more readily available.

The autobiography as told to Câmara does not cover the complete life of Ignatius. It begins abruptly in 1521 at the great turning point in the saint's life—his injury in the battle of Pamplona when the French occupied that town and attacked its citadel. It then spans the next seventeen years up to the arrival of Ignatius and his early companions in Rome and their first difficulties and activities in the Eternal City. These years are the central years of Ignatius's life. They are the years, as we have already indicated, that open with his

3. The earliest manuscripts are described and evaluated in *FN,* I, 331ff. The text itself as well as the early Latin translation by Father Annibal du Coudray is in ibid., I, 354–507.

4. *St. Ignatius' Own Story* (Chicago, 1956). We might also note the excellent French edition, *Le récit du pèlerin,* ed. A. Thiry, S.J. (Bruges, 1956).

religious conversion and that witness his spiritual growth. They are the years of pilgrimage, to use his own designation, of active travel and searching, and of interior progress in the Christian life. They are the years of preparation for the establishment of the great religious order he will found and for its dynamic thrust in the turbulent Europe and the expanding world of his day. Thus we have only a phase of Ignatius's long life, but it is a most substantial phase, and it is unquestionably a most meaningful and determinant one. If, in the words of Teilhard de Chardin, "nothing is comprehensible except through its history," Ignatius's narrative of the events of these formative and decisive years is essential for our understanding of him and his heritage. The fact that he left us this particular "testament" confirms it. Yet the modern reader, far removed from the milieu of the early Society of Jesus, has need perhaps for some supplementary data, for a brief description of the total setting of Ignatius's pilgrim years as well as for clarification of certain references tersely made in the autobiography. In our introduction and notes we have tried to supply this need and to enhance the intelligibility and historical value of the document at hand.

Ignatius was born in 1491 of a noble Basque family in the province of Guipuzcoa in the old kingdom of Castile. He was the youngest of thirteen children. The site of the family property and castle, not far from the town of Azpeitia, was called Loyola, and Ignatius originally was known as Iñigo Lopez de Loyola. He assumed the name Ignatius much later in his life during his Paris years, probably out of devotion to the early father, St. Ignatius of Antioch. (Ignatius is not simply the Latin form for Iñigo.) Long before this occurred, however, Ignatius was a youthful courtier, a swaggering caballero, and a soldier in the service of the Spanish king. He was in the household of the royal treasurer of Spain, Juan Velazquez de Cuellar, from about 1507 to 1517. After that he joined the forces of the Duke of Nájera, then viceroy of Navarre and in charge of its defense. That region along the Pyrenees in northern Spain which King Ferdinand had conquered and annexed in 1512 stood vulnerable to

French attack at this time, and in the spring of 1521 the invasion came. It was an early operation in the long war between Francis I of France and the Holy Roman Emperor Charles V that reopened in 1521. (Charles V was also king of Spain, having succeeded his grandfather Ferdinand in 1516.) In the course of the invasion the French occupied the city of Pamplona in Navarre, but the Spanish garrison in the citadel stubbornly held out. Ignatius was foremost among the defenders and was severely wounded in the French bombardment of the citadel on May 20, 1521. The autobiography, as we noted above, begins at this point in his life.

After the battle the French brought him back to the family castle at Loyola where he had a painful and difficult convalescence. When his health began to improve toward late summer he was given some religious books to read instead of the chivalrous romances he would have preferred. These books were two widely read medieval works that had been translated into Spanish and published in Spain quite a few years before: *The Life of Christ* by a German Carthusian, Ludolph of Saxony, and a collection of saints' lives known as *The Golden Legend* by a thirteenth-century Dominican writer, Jacopo de Voragine.[5] Ignatius's conversion began with his reading and pondering the pages of these hefty tomes, and he stands forth indeed as one of the classic examples of the man profoundly influenced by what he has read—a striking witness to the power of a book. The possibility of another way of life and of another kind of achievement than any he had heretofore known or dreamed of now opened up for the convalescent. He was torn between two romantic ideals, and he began, as he says, "to recognize the difference between the spirits that agitated him." He finally resolved to forsake his worldly desires and ambitions and to do great deeds like the saints for the love of God. He decided to go as a penitent and pilgrim to Jerusalem as soon as he was able.

5. On these books and their influence on Ignatius, see Leturia, *Iñigo de Loyola,* pp. 83ff.; and Hugo Rahner, S.J., *The Spirituality of St. Ignatius Loyola,* trans. F. J. Smith, S.J. (Westminster, Md., 1953), pp. 22ff.

But his own words tell us this story better than any sketch we can give. We shall simply indicate the main course of the action and underscore some of its features. He did set out from Loyola in early 1522 and went to the shrine of Our Lady at Montserrat in Catalonia and thence to the nearby town of Manresa, where he spent several months. His experiences there were of the utmost importance. He describes them at some length in the autobiography (Chapter 3), and he frequently extolled the Manresa period as his "primitive church." In Jesuit tradition it has always been viewed as a decisive stage in his career. With God instructing him like a schoolmaster, as Ignatius tells us, his mind was enlightened, his understanding immeasurably deepened. Ignatius the caballero was transformed into the soldier of Christ in the spiritual sense of that ancient term, and his apostolate —his service under the standard of Christ the Eternal King—began.[6] He was still to be the pilgrim whose progress would continue, but his eyes had been opened, and his future course was set.

He made the journey to Jerusalem by way of Rome and Venice in 1523. The Franciscan guardians of the holy places, however, rejected his plea to remain among them, and he returned to Spain early the next year. He had decided now to study, that is, to pursue a formal education, "so he would be able to help souls," as he expresses it. And so began a long academic interlude commencing with Latin instruction at Barcelona in 1524 and climaxed by his acquisition of a master of arts at Paris in 1534. Ignatius's studies carried him to some famous schools, and he was certainly exposed during these years to the powerful intellectual and religious currents that were then stirring Europe. These were years of exceptional ferment and agitation. The impact of overseas discovery and expansion was being fully felt, tension and conflict among the major states

6. See Rahner, *Spirituality of St. Ignatius Loyola,* pp. 46 ff. Rahner's view of Ignatius's mystical illumination at Manresa and the sudden transformation wrought is criticized—and counterbalanced—in H. O. Evennett, *The Spirit of the Counter-Reformation,* ed. John Bossy (Cambridge, 1968), pp. 51–64, 126–30, where greater emphasis is placed on the many influences that bore upon him and on a more gradual and historical "spiritual formation."

were prolonged and acute, the exhilarating challenge and influence of humanism had reached its peak, and the religious crisis precipitated by Luther's protest and rebellion at Wittenberg became even more serious and divisive. No matter how dedicated he was to his spiritual vocation or his studies, Ignatius could hardly have failed to have been aware of the problems and issues of the world about him and to have been marked himself by the forces that were molding it. He has very little to say about these historic factors in the autobiography; but obviously they are the broader context of his life and mission, and we can be sure they played a part in his development.

From Barcelona he passed to the University of Alcalá in 1526 and in the following year to the University of Salamanca—the newest and oldest of Spain's great centers of learning. In both places, however, he had serious trouble with the Inquisition, and, suspected of being an *alumbrado,* he was investigated and confined. He tells us quite a bit about these encounters in the autobiography (Chapters 6 and 7). To escape further interference by the Inquisition in Spain, in early 1528 he went to Paris, where he first entered the austere college of Montaigu and later shifted to the more liberal college of Sainte-Barbe. He remained in Paris until 1535, completing his arts course at Sainte-Barbe and then studying theology for over a year with the Dominicans on the rue Saint-Jacques. The Paris years are significant both for the education of Ignatius and for the future Society of Jesus.[7] It was there he gathered the companions with whom he would later form the new religious order. Their comradeship in a spiritual life and, specifically, the intention they expressed and the vows they took in a chapel on Montmartre on August 15, 1534 (to which Ignatius briefly alludes at the end of Chapter 8), prefigure the Society and prepare the way for its foundation. With their studies coming to an end, Ignatius and his friends resolved to go to Jerusalem and labor for the conversion of the Turks. If that

7. On the Paris years see especially Robert Rouquette, S.J., "Ignace de Loyola dans le Paris intellectual du XVIe siècle," *Études* 290 (1956): 18–40; and H. Bernard-Maître, S.J., "Les fondateurs de la Compagnie de Jésus et l'humanisme parisien de la Renaissance," *Nouvelle revue théologique* 72 (1950): 811–33.

should not prove possible, they intended then to go to Rome and put themselves at the disposal of the pope, "so that he might make use of them wherever he thought it would be to the greater glory of God and the service of souls."

In the spring of 1535 Ignatius returned to Spain, where he spent a few months in his native Guipuzcoa and showed himself a very active reformer. At the end of the year he left for Italy, making his way to Venice and an eventual rendezvous with his friends from Paris. Nine companions joined him there at the beginning of 1537. This was the first leg of their journey to the Holy Land, but, unable to get a ship out of Venice for the East, they departed for Rome after a year to offer their services to the pope. Ignatius's pilgrimage, so to speak, was over. He had arrived at his goal, and his new apostolate, his mission as founder and director of a dynamic order, was about to begin. He ends his autobiographical narrative at this point, and it is a logical terminus for the personal account he was revealing to his sons. What followed after his arrival in Rome was better known, part of the *res gestae* of the nascent Society of Jesus, the knowledge of which was shared by a widening circle. "Master Nadal can recount the rest," Ignatius tells Câmara as he concludes his story.

The Rome Ignatius and his friends had come to in 1538 was the Rome of Paul III, the Farnese pope whose long pontificate began nearly four years before. Though the city seemed "exceedingly barren of good fruit and abundant in bad," as Ignatius observed,[8] the forces making for Catholic reform and renewal were slowly gathering under papal auspices. Paul III's tenure as successor of Peter opened a new chapter in the history of the Catholic church.[9] He brought many of the most able and dedicated Catholic reformers to Rome and infused new life and leadership into the papal administration. From the start he sought to convene the General Council that so many desired to deal with the grave problems confronting

8. In the letter to Isabel Roser referred to below. See Appendix I.
9. See John C. Olin, *The Catholic Reformation: Savonarola to Ignatius Loyola* (New York, 1969), pp. 182ff. Paul III's pontificate extended from 1534 to 1549.

the church, and he did so finally at Trent in late 1545. He took many other measures to stem the tide of heresy and disruption and to restore and revivify religious life. In all these events Ignatius and the Jesuits were to play an outstanding part and were to become perhaps the most important agents of Catholic revival in this troubled age. The unheralded arrival of these "pilgrim priests" in the Eternal City at this propitious time was then itself an event of historic moment.

In a letter to an old friend and benefactress in Barcelona, Isabel Roser, Ignatius has given us an interesting account of the initial months in Rome.[10] He and his band were at first the object of suspicion and hostility, "the most severe persecution," Ignatius calls it. But when they gained the support of Cardinal Gasparo Contarini, a very eminent man and the leader of the reform party at Rome, and of the pope himself whom Ignatius visited at Frascati, they were exhonerated and could henceforth carry on their activities with greater freedom. These activities were to preach, instruct children, hear confessions, give the spiritual exercises that Ignatius had devised and elaborated over the years since his conversion, and carry out various works of charity. Paul III assigned two of Ignatius's companions—Peter Faber and Diego Lainez—to teach theology at the Sapienza, the papal college in Rome, and soon other prelates also were requesting their services. They were even being sought to go to the Indies. Diego de Gouvea, the principal of Sainte-Barbe in Paris, had recommended them to the Portuguese king with this in mind, and the first steps were already being taken which would lead to the departure of Francis Xavier for Lisbon in early 1540 and the beginning of the great Jesuit missionary venture.[11]

Up to this point Ignatius had not entertained the idea of founding a religious order. He and his companions were united simply by their common purpose and zeal. They were priests and masters of arts from Paris, determined to serve Christ and souls. The new range

10. This letter, dated December 19, 1538, is in Appendix I. It confirms and supplements the final pages of the autobiography.
11. See Appendix II.

and character of their activities, however, suggested a more formal status and organization. In the spring of 1539 the group in Rome discussed very thoroughly the questions involved in such organization, and they drew up a brief statement of their plans for official recognition and approval.[12] This document, the original sketch or *prima summa* of the Society of Jesus, was submitted to the pope that summer through the good offices of Cardinal Contarini. Paul gave preliminary approval in September, but it was another full year before the formal bull of approbation, *Regimini militantis ecclesiae,* was issued. A delay had been caused by opposition in the Roman curia to the revolutionary concept of a religious order the proposal of Ignatius and his friends represented.

The events of 1539–40 nevertheless brought the Society of Jesus into being, and this indeed was the climax, the fruition of Ignatius's previous life and activities. New members rapidly joined the ranks, the companions soon began to disperse on various missions at the behest of the pope, and the far-flung enterprises of the Society commenced. Of the original band Ignatius alone stayed in Rome to direct the fast-growing order. He was chosen as the *prepositus* or general in April 1541, and he remained at this post until his death on July 31, 1556. The last fifteen years of his life were more sedentary than the previous twenty we have discussed. He was occupied with the routine and wearisome tasks of administration, but also with the inauguration and development of the activities of a Society of over 1,000 members laboring in every part of the world. He drafted the order's constitutions; he counseled and instructed its members in an immense correspondence; he presided over the establishment of its schools and colleges throughout Europe; he dispatched his sons to a hundred fruitful tasks. He saw indeed the fulfillment of a mission far greater than any he had dreamed of in the castle of Loyola.

There are two aspects of Ignatius's story that deserve further

12. James Brodrick, S.J., *The Origin of the Jesuits* (New York, 1940), pp. 68ff. This important statement is given in Appendix III.

comment in this Introduction. One concerns the specific nature of his religious experience and orientation; the other pertains to its historical character and significance. These topics are interrelated, for Ignatius's conversion and spiritual development occurred in the context of history and was influenced by it, and it had, in turn, an impact on history because of its relevance to the currents and needs of the time. The man and the hour appear to have met in the fullest sense of the expression in the case of Ignatius Loyola. We shall, however, separate the two for the moment and first speak of the interior or personal side of the story and then of its broader historical aspect.

What was the experience Ignatius underwent and the change wrought in him in the days of his convalescence at Loyola and down through his visit to Montserrat and his months at Manresa? The autobiography gives a fairly extended account of all of this, and we have already noted above some of the salient features of his transformation. What else can we say in analyzing this conversion experience? We cannot fail to observe that it was remarkably action-centered and dynamic. Ignatius above all wanted to *do* something for the glory of God out of love for God. Inspired by the deeds of the saints, he now wished to live and work in the service of Christ the King. His resolve was clarified and purified as he progressed along his pilgrim's way, but from beginning to end it was a determination to accomplish notable deeds, to lead a life of active service. This has often been viewed as the transposition of an ideal of chivalry or knightly service to the religious realm. This may well be the case, but acknowledging that actually tells us little about the reason for it or the intensity of Ignatius's new resolve or the way it did transform and energize his life. Ignatius himself saw God directing and enlightening him, and Jesuit tradition has always accepted the reality of divine inspiration in his case, of God's "mystical invasion" of his soul, to quote Hugo Rahner.[13] There is no doubt that he was a man overwhelmed by a perception of the divine, and it is perhaps quite

13. Rahner, *Spirituality of St. Ignatius Loyola,* p. 47.

correct to view him as a mystic.[14] Yet there is need or, at least, room for a further explanation of what it was he received or comprehended and how it impelled him to action.

The autobiography does not entirely satisfy us on this score. In one sense this is understandable, for Ignatius in his narrative was speaking to those in the Society of Jesus who had already been won to his ideal of active service and had been oriented toward it and trained for it through the spiritual exercises. It is the latter instrument, which H. O. Evennett has characterized as "the systematised, de-mysticised quintessence of the process of Ignatius's own conversion and purposeful change of life," that can shed some light.[15] The spiritual exercises are a handbook compiled by Ignatius, but even more they are a structured and well-ordered procedure of prayer, meditation, and self-examination to be undergone. The written text or book actually consists of an outline and directives for the guidance of the person giving the exercises. Ignatius drew them from his own experience and set them down for the help of others. There are two exercises in particular that stand out: the meditation on the kingdom of Christ and the meditation on the two standards.[16] Derived from his convalescent reading at Loyola, their fundamental importance has always been recognized, and they can rightly be called an essential part of Ignatius's "vision of the universe and of man."[17]

Ignatius saw the world as the scene of conflict between Christ and Satan, each summoning and striving to attract all men to his standard. It was strictly a spiritual conflict for the souls of men, but it was the real issue that confronted all, the true meaning of the human drama. The call of Christ the Eternal King, of course, was the sum-

14. He is the first to be considered in E. Allison Peers, *Studies of the Spanish Mystics,* 4 vols. (London, 1927–35), I, 1–30.

15. Evennett, *Counter-Reformation,* p. 45. There are several English editions of the spiritual exercises, the best text being *The Spiritual Exercises of St. Ignatius,* trans. Louis J. Puhl, S.J. (Westminster, Md., 1951, 2d ed. Chicago, n.d.).

16. *Spiritual Exercises,* 2d ed., pp. 43–45, 60–62. On the importance of these two meditations see Rahner, *Spirituality of St. Ignatius Loyola,* pp. 34–40.

17. Jean Danielou, S.J., "The Ignatian Vision of the Universe and of Man," *Cross Currents,* Vol. 4, No. 4 (Fall 1954), pp. 357–66.

mons that deserved our response, and all were asked to work with Christ in winning souls and conquering the world.

To all His summons goes forth, and to each one in particular He addresses the words: "It is my will to conquer the whole world and all my enemies, and thus to enter into the glory of my Father. Therefore, whoever wishes to join me in this enterprise must be willing to labor with me, that by following me in suffering, he may follow me in glory."[18]

Ignatius's conversion, in short, was the perception of this design, and his new life was the response to the challenge of the Eternal King.

Much more can certainly be said about the "vision" and thought and spirituality of Ignatius Loyola, and there is, indeed, an extensive literature on the subject.[19] The fundamentals, nevertheless, seem simple and clear. Ignatius came to view the world in the dramatic terms of a sacred history in which man was called to action by a God who is ever active in creation, a *deus operarius,* "who works and labors for me in all creatures upon the face of the earth."[20] Each was called to discern the universal struggle and choose his side, to enter the spiritual combat, and to labor with Christ. The whole key was the decisive commitment and engagement under the standard of Christ, and it involved that prior "discernment of spirits" which Ignatius himself had first experienced while he convalesced at Loyola. The religious life thus became the purposeful active life, and Ignatius's conversion the source of intense activity. He truly became, in the memorable phrase of Nadal, "the contemplative in action."[21]

The historical significance of this is two-fold. It is reflective or characteristic of the times, and it had, in turn, major consequences

18. *Spiritual Exercises,* 2d ed., p. 44.
19. In addition to the works already cited above, see Joseph de Guibert, S.J., *The Jesuits, Their Spiritual Doctrine and Practice,* trans. William J. Young, S.J. (Chicago, 1964); and Hugo Rahner, S.J., *Ignatius the Theologian,* trans. Michael Barry (New York, 1968).
20. *Spiritual Exercises* 2d ed., p. 103. See also Danielou, *"Ignatian Vision of the Universe,"* p. 358.
21. Nadal's term is quoted and discussed in Danielou, "Ignatian Vision of the Universe," p. 364; and in the superb essay by Maurice Giuliani, S.J., "Finding God in All Things," in *Finding God in All Things, Essays in Ignatian Spirituality Selected from Christus,* trans. William J. Young, S.J. (Chicago, 1958), p. 23.

on the renewal and resurgence of Catholicism in the sixteenth century. The latter flowed, in part at least, from the former. Ignatius's experience had consequences because there was a rapport between it and the temper, as well as the needs, of the age. However one may view its ultimate source or enduring relevance, it was an experience that epitomized many of the spiritual tendencies then prominent. It was an interior conversion, it centered on Christ, it emphasized self-discipline, it was marked by independence of spirit and individuality, it overflowed into a highly active apostolate. It bridged the gap between a religious dedication and a life of service in the world. It was an experience fully situated in the context of events, and it led by its very nature to an even deeper involvement in events. This total historicity of Ignatius's experience, it would seem, goes far to account for the amazing force and attraction it had.

It has frequently been observed that Ignatius and the Jesuits mark a new stage or development in Catholic spirituality: a break with older medieval forms of piety and monasticism and the expression of a concept of the religious life more relevant to the times, more streamlined, so to speak, more engaged, more dynamic. Such is the main theme in H. O. Evennett's penetrating study *The Spirit of the Counter-Reformation,* where Ignatius's experience and foundation are linked to the influence of the *Devotio moderna* and are seen to represent par excellence the spirit of adaptation and renewal that characterized the Catholic reformation. The concise statement of purpose and organization which Ignatius and his companions drew up for their Society in 1539 is indeed a clear witness of this. It is hard today to appreciate, says Evennett, how "revolutionary" their enterprise then appeared.[22] We can, however, take some measure of the deeds that were done, and we know that they had their beginning and their source in the spiritual adventure of a Spanish knight who has left us an account of his pilgrim years.

22. Evennett, *Counter-Reformation,* p. 74. In addition to Evennett's analysis of the Society in his chapter 4, see also David Knowles, *From Pachomius to Ignatius* (Oxford, 1966), pp. 61–68.

Preface of Father Luis Gonçalves da Câmara

One Friday morning, the fourth of August and the vigil of our Lady of the Snows, in the year 1553, while the Father was in the garden next to the house or residence known as the Duke's, I began to give him an account of some of the inner concerns of my soul.[1] Among other things I spoke to him of vainglory. As a remedy the Father told me to refer all my affairs frequently to God, striving to offer Him all the good I found in myself, recognizing it as His and giving Him thanks for it. He spoke to me about this in a manner that greatly consoled me so that I could not restrain my tears. The Father then told me how he had striven against this vice for two years, so much so that when he embarked from Barcelona for Jerusalem, he did not dare tell anyone that he was going to Jerusalem; and so he had acted in other similar instances. Moreover, he added that thereafter he had felt great peace in his soul. An hour or two after this we went to eat. While Master Polanco and I were eating with him, the Father said that Master Nadal and others of the Society had often asked a favor of him, but he had never decided about it. But that after having spoken to me, when he retired to his room, he had a great desire

1. The site was the Jesuit residence in Rome which today adjoins the Church of the Gesù. The Duke's residence is a reference to the apartment occupied by St. Francis Borgia, the Duke of Gandia and a member of the new Society, when he visited Rome a few years before. The Father, of course, is St. Ignatius.

15

and inclination to do it, and (speaking in a manner that showed that God had enlightened him as to his duty to do so) he had fully decided to reveal all that had occurred in his soul until now. He had also decided that I should be the one to whom he would reveal these things.

The Father was very ill at that time and never used to promise himself a single day of life. Whenever someone would say, "I will do this two weeks from now or a week from now," the Father would always say with amazement, "What, do you think you will live that long?" And yet this time he said that he expected to live three or four months to finish this business. The next day I spoke to him, asking when he wished us to begin; he replied that I should remind him of it each day (I don't remember how many days) until he was ready. But as his duties did not allow him time for it, he told me later to remind him each Sunday. So in September (I don't remember the day) the Father called me and began to tell me about his whole life and his youthful escapades, clearly and distinctly and with all their circumstances.[2] Later in the same month he called me three or four times and carried his story down to his stay at Manresa, as one may see by the change in the script.

The Father's narrative manner is the same that he uses in everything. He speaks with such clarity that he seems to make everything that has passed present to his listener. Therefore, it was not necessary to ask him anything because the Father remembered to tell everything relevant to an understanding of his story. Then, without saying anything to the Father, I went immediately to write it down, first in notes by my own hand and later at greater length, as it is now written. I have striven not to put down any word except those that I heard from the Father, but in some things I fear I have failed because, in order not to depart from the Father's words, I have not been able to explain clearly the intent of some of them. Thus I wrote,

2. The story of Ignatius's early life and youthful escapades however is missing in the texts we have. Either it was suppressed in later renditions or, more likely, Câmara did not see fit to pass it on.

as I said above, until September 1553, but from then until Father Nadal came on October 18, 1554, the Father was always excusing himself because of some illness or various matters that arose, saying to me, "When such and such business is finished, remind me of it"; and when it was finished and I reminded him of it, he would say, "We are now into this other matter; when it is finished, remind me of it."

When Father Nadal came, he was very pleased that it was begun and bade me to urge the Father, telling me many times that the Father could do nothing of greater benefit for the Society than this and that this was truly to found the Society. He himself spoke to the Father many times in this way. The Father told me to remind him of it when the business of endowing the College was finished, but after it was done, when the affair of Prester John was finished and the mail was to go.[3] We began to continue the story on the ninth of March, but Pope Julius III began to be in danger of death at that time and died on the twenty-third, so the Father postponed the matter until the succession of another pope. Pope Marcellus succeeded, but he also fell ill immediately and died. The Father delayed until the elevation of Pope Paul IV and afterwards, because of the great heat and his many affairs, postponed it continually until the twenty-first of September when the question of sending me to Spain began to be discussed. For this reason I strongly urged the Father to fulfill his promise to me. So then he arranged to do so for the morning of the twenty-second in the Red Tower. When I finished saying mass, I presented myself to him to ask if it was time.

He replied that I should wait for him in the Red Tower so that when he arrived, I would be there. I realized that I would have to wait for him a long time in that place. While I was standing in a hallway speaking with a brother who had asked me something, the Father came along and reproved me because, failing in obedience,

3. The College referred to is the famous Roman College of the Society which had been opened in 1551. The affair of Prester John is the business of organizing a mission to go to Ethiopia whose ruler was thought to be the legendary Christian monarch Prester John.

I had not waited for him in the Red Tower. He did not want to do anything that whole day. Later we were very insistent with him. So he returned to the Red Tower and dictated, walking up and down as he had always done before. In order to observe his face I kept coming a little closer to him, but the Father said to me, "Keep the rule." When, forgetting his warning, I came up to him again, doing this two or three times, the Father repeated the same warning and left. At length he returned to the same Tower and finished dictating to me what has been written here. But, as I was for some time on the point of undertaking my journey (the eve of my departure was the last day on which the Father spoke to me about this matter), I could not set everything down in full in Rome. In Genoa, not having a Spanish scribe, I dictated in Italian whatever I had brought in note form from Rome. I finished writing at Genoa in December 1555.

In lecto decumbens, dum ad recreandum
animum Christi domini vitam et exem=
pla Sanctorum euoluit, diuinarum virtutum
imitatione exardescens, ad Deum conuertitur.

4

Ignatius reading as a convalescent at Loyola.

CHAPTER I

Convalescence and Conversion
(May 1521–February 1522)

Until the age of twenty-six he was a man given over to vanities of the world; with a great and vain desire to win fame he delighted especially in the exercise of arms.[1] Once when he was in a fortress that the French were attacking, although all the others saw clearly that they could not defend themselves and were of the opinion that they should surrender provided their lives were spared, he gave so many reasons to the commander that he persuaded him at last to defend it; this was contrary to the views of all the knights, but they were encouraged by his valor and energy. When the day arrived on which the bombardment was expected, he confessed to one of his companions in arms. After the bombardment had lasted a good while, a shot hit him in the leg, breaking it completely; since the ball passed through both legs, the other one was also badly damaged.

When he fell, the defenders of the fortress surrendered immediately to the French who, having taken possession of it, treated the wounded man very well, with courtesy and kindness. After he had been in Pamplona for twelve or fifteen days, they carried him on a

---

1. The age given in the opening line is an error. Most probably Ignatius was born in 1491, and his age at this time would have been twenty-nine or thirty. The attack he speaks of in the next sentence was the French attack on the citadel of Pamplona in Spanish Navarre, and it occurred in May 1521.

litter to his own country where he was very ill. All the doctors and surgeons who were summoned from many places decided that the leg ought to be broken again and the bones reset because they had been badly set the first time or had been broken on the road and were out of place and could not heal. This butchery was done again; during it, as in all the others he suffered before or since, he never spoke a word nor showed any sign of pain other than to clench his fists.

Yet he continued to get worse, not being able to eat and showing the other indications that are usually signs of death. When the feast of St. John came, because the doctors had very little confidence in his health, he was advised to confess; he received the sacraments on the vigil of Sts. Peter and Paul. The doctors said that if he did not feel better by midnight, he could consider himself dead. As the sick man had devotion to St. Peter, Our Lord willed that he should begin to improve that very midnight. His improvement proceeded so quickly that some days later it was decided that he was out of danger of death.

As his bones knit together, one bone below the knee remained on top of another, shortening his leg. The bone protruded so much that it was an ugly sight. He was unable to abide it because he was determined to follow the world and he thought that it would deform him; he asked the surgeons if it could be cut away. They said that indeed it could be cut away, but that the pain would be greater than all those that he had suffered, because it was already healed and it would take some time to cut it. Yet he was determined to make himself a martyr to his own pleasure. His older brother was astounded and said that he himself would not dare to suffer such pain, but the wounded man endured it with his customary patience.

After the flesh and excess bone were cut away, means were taken so the leg would not be so short; many ointments were applied to it, and, as it was stretched continually with instruments, he suffered martyrdom for many days. But Our Lord was restoring his health, and he was getting well. In everything else he was healthy except that he could not stand easily on his leg and had to stay in bed. As he was much given to reading worldly and fictitious books, usually called books of chivalry, when he felt better he asked to be given some of them to pass the time. But in that house none of those that he usually read could be found, so they gave him a Life of Christ and a book of the lives of the saints in Spanish.[2]

As he read them over many times, he became rather fond of what he found written there. Putting his reading aside, he sometimes stopped to think about the things he had read and at other times about the things of the world that he used to think about before. Of the many vain things that presented themselves to him, one took such a hold on his heart that he was absorbed in thinking about it for two or three or four hours without realizing it: he imagined what he would do in the service of a certain lady, the means he would take so he could go to the country where she lived, the verses, the words he would say to her, the deeds of arms he would do in her service. He became so conceited with this that he did not consider how impossible it would be because the lady was not of the lower nobility nor a countess nor a duchess, but her station was higher than any of these.[3]

Nevertheless, Our Lord assisted him, causing other thoughts that arose from the things he read to follow these. While reading the life of Our Lord and of the saints, he stopped to think, reasoning within himself, "What if I should do what St. Francis did, what St. Dominic did?" So he pondered over many things that he found to be good, always proposing to himself what was difficult and serious, and as he proposed them, they seemed to him easy to accomplish. But his every thought was to say to himself, "St. Dominic did this, therefore, I have to do it. St. Francis did this, therefore, I have to do it." These thoughts also lasted a good while, but when other matters intervened, the worldly thoughts mentioned above returned, and he also

2. See Introduction, p. 5.
3. There is considerable speculation about the identity of this lady. Leturia, *Iñigo de Loyola*, pp. 59–60, suggests that it was the Princess Catherine, the young and beautiful sister of King Charles of Spain, whom Ignatius may have seen at Valladolid in 1518. She later married John III of Portugal.

spent much time on them. This succession of such diverse thoughts, either of the worldly deeds he wished to achieve or of the deeds of God that came to his imagination, lasted for a long time, and he always dwelt at length on the thought before him, until he tired of it and put it aside and turned to other matters.

Yet there was this difference. When he was thinking about the things of the world, he took much delight in them, but afterwards, when he was tired and put them aside, he found that he was dry and discontented. But when he thought of going to Jerusalem, barefoot and eating nothing but herbs and undergoing all the other rigors that he saw the saints had endured, not only was he consoled when he had these thoughts, but even after putting them aside, he remained content and happy. He did not wonder, however, at this; nor did he stop to ponder the difference until one time his eyes were opened a little, and he began to marvel at the difference and to reflect upon it, realizing from experience that some thoughts left him sad and others happy. Little by little he came to recognize the difference between the spirits that agitated him, one from the demon, the other from God.

From this reading he obtained not a little insight, and he began to think more earnestly about his past life and about the great need he had to do penance for it. At this point the desire to imitate the saints came to him, though he gave no thought to the circumstances, but only promised with God's grace to do as they had done. All he wanted to do was to go to Jerusalem as soon as he recovered, as mentioned above, performing all the disciplines and abstinences which a generous soul, inflamed by God, usually wants to do.

And so he began to forget the thoughts of the past with these holy desires he had, and they were confirmed by a vision in this manner. One night while he was awake, he saw clearly an image of Our Lady with the holy child Jesus. From this sight he received for a considerable time very great consolation, and he was left with such loathing for his whole past life and especially for the things of the flesh, that it seemed that all the fantasies he had previously pictured in his mind were driven from it. Thus from that hour until August 1553 when this was written, he never gave the slightest consent to the things of the flesh. For this reason the vision may be considered the work of God, although he did not dare to claim it nor to say more than to affirm the above. But his brother and the rest of the household knew from his exterior the change that had been working inwardly in his soul.

Without any cares he persevered in his reading and his good intentions, and he spent all his time in conversation with members of the household, speaking about the things of God. In so doing he benefited their souls. Taking great pleasure in those books, the idea came to him to excerpt in brief some of the more essential things from the life of Christ and the saints; so with great diligence (because he was now beginning to be up and about the house a bit) he set himself to write a book in a good hand (because he was a very fine penman), using red ink for the words of Christ, blue ink for those of Our Lady, and polished and lined paper. Part of his time was spent in writing and part in prayer. The greatest consolation he received was to look at the sky and the stars, which he often did and for a long time, because as a result he felt within himself a very great desire to serve Our Lord. He often thought about his intention and wished to be healed completely now so he could take the road.

Considering what he would do after he returned from Jerusalem, he decided to ask to enter the Carthusian house in Seville so he could always live as a penitent; nor would he say who he was so they would hold him in scant esteem, and there he would eat nothing but herbs. But when he thought again of the penances he wished to do as he went about the world, the desire to enter the Carthusians cooled; he feared that he would not be able to give vent to the hatred that he had conceived against himself. Still he ordered one of the household servants who was going to Burgos to get information about the rule of the Carthusians, and the information he obtained about it seemed good. But for the reason mentioned above and because he was wholly absorbed in the journey he was planning soon to make and because that matter did not have to be dealt with until his return, he stopped thinking about it so much. Finding now that he had some strength, it seemed to him that the time to depart had come, and he said to his brother, "Sir, the Duke of Nájera, as you know, is aware that I am well. It will be good for me to go to Navarrete."[4] (The duke was there at that time.) His brother took him from one room to another and with many protestations begged him not to throw himself away and to consider what hopes had been placed in him and what he could become and he advanced other similar arguments, all with the purpose of dissuading him from his good intention. But he answered in such a way that, without departing from the truth, for he was now very scrupulous about that, he evaded his brother.

4. The Duke of Nájera was the viceroy of Navarre at this time. It was in his service that Ignatius was employed as a soldier and had fought at Pamplona. Navarrete, where the Duke had a residence, is about fifty miles to the south of Loyola.

E domo & cognatione sua exit, rectaque
ad Virginis templum famulis redire
iussis, in Montem Serratum contendit.

7

Ignatius setting out from Loyola on his pilgrimage.

CHAPTER 2

The Pilgrim Sets Out
(March 1522)

And so he set out riding on a mule. On the road he persuaded his other brother who wanted to accompany him as far as Oñate to keep a vigil with him at Our Lady of Aránzazu. That night he prayed there for new strength for his journey. He left his brother in Oñate at the home of a sister he was going to visit and went on to Navarrete. Remembering that a few ducats were owed him at the duke's household, he thought it would be well to collect them; for this purpose he wrote out a bill for the treasurer. The treasurer said that he did not have any money, but when the duke learned of it, he said that he might default in everything else, but money should not be lacking for Loyola. The duke wanted to give him a good position, if he would accept it, because of the reputation he had earned in the past. He collected the money, ordered it to be distributed among certain persons to whom he felt indebted, and gave part of it for a statue of Our Lady that was poorly adorned, so it could be better dressed and decorated. Then saying goodbye to two servants who had come with him, he set out alone on his mule from Navarrete for Montserrat.[1]

1. It was a long and arduous journey of over 300 miles that lay before Ignatius. His route was across northern Spain in the valley of the Ebro via Saragossa and Lerida to the famous shrine of Our Lady at Montserrat in Catalonia.

On the way something happened to him which it will be good to record, so one may understand how Our Lord dealt with his soul, which was still blind, though greatly desirous of serving Him in every way he knew. Thus, no longer so much concerned to do satisfaction for his sins, but to please and placate God, he decided to do great penances. When he remembered some penance that the saints had done, he determined to do the same and even more. From these thoughts he took all his consolation. He did not dwell on any interior thing, nor did he know what humility was or charity or patience or discretion to regulate and measure these virtues. Without considering any more particular circumstance, his every intention was to do these great external works because the saints had done so for the glory of God.

As he was going on his way, then, a Moor riding on a mule came up to him, and they went on talking together. They began to talk about Our Lady, and the Moor said it seemed to him that the Virgin had indeed conceived without a man, but he could not believe that she remained a virgin after giving birth. In support of this he cited the natural reasons that suggested themselves to him. The pilgrim,[2] in spite of the many reasons he gave him, could not dissuade him from this opinion. The Moor then went on ahead so rapidly that he lost sight of him, and he was left to think about what had transpired with the Moor. Various emotions came over him and caused discontent in his soul, as it seemed to him that he had not done his duty. This also aroused his indignation against the Moor, for he thought that he had done wrong in allowing the Moor to say such things about Our Lady and that he was obliged to defend her honor. A desire came over him to go in search of the Moor and strike him with his dagger for what he had said. He struggled with this conflict of desires for a long time, uncertain to the end as to what he was obliged to do. The Moor, who had gone on ahead, had told him that

---

2. Ignatius will hereafter refer to himself in the autobiography as the pilgrim, *el peregrino.*

he was going to a place on the same road a little farther on, very near the highway, though the highway did not pass through the place.

Tired of examining what would be best to do and not finding any guiding principle, he decided as follows, to let the mule go with the reins slack as far as the place where the road separated. If the mule took the village road, he would seek out the Moor and strike him; if the mule did not go toward the village but kept on the highway, he would let him be. He did as he proposed. Although the village was little more than thirty or forty paces away, and the road to it was very broad and very good, Our Lord willed that the mule took the highway and not the village road. Coming to a large town before Montserrat, he wanted to buy there the clothing he had decided to wear when he went to Jerusalem. He bought cloth from which sacks were usually made, loosely woven and very prickly. Then he ordered a long garment reaching to his feet to be made from it. He bought a pilgrim's staff and a small gourd and put everything up front on the mule's saddle.

He went on his way to Montserrat, thinking as always about the deeds he would do for the love of God. As his mind was full of ideas from Amadis of Gaul and such books, some things similar to those came to mind.[3] Thus he decided to watch over his arms all one night, without sitting down or going to bed, but standing a while and kneeling a while, before the altar of Our Lady of Montserrat where he had resolved to leave his clothing and dress himself in the armor of Christ. Leaving this place then he went on, thinking as usual about his intentions. After arriving at Montserrat, he said a prayer and arranged for a confessor. He made a general confession in writing which lasted three days. He arranged with the confessor to take his mule and to place his sword and his dagger in the church on the altar

3. Amadis of Gaul, a legendary knight and model of chivalry, was the hero of an extensive prose romance that was very popular and widely published in Spain in the sixteenth century. On this particular passage see the interesting article by John F. Wickham, S.J., "The Worldly Ideal of Iñigo Loyola," *Thought*, Vol. 29, No. 113 (Summer 1954), pp. 209–36.

of Our Lady. This was the first man to whom he revealed his deci-sion, because until then he had not revealed it to any confessor.[4]

On the eve of the feast of Our Lady in March in the year 1522, he went at night as secretly as he could to a poor man, and stripping off all his garments he gave them to the poor man and dressed himself in his desired clothing and went to kneel before the altar of Our Lady. At times in this way, at other times standing, with his pilgrim's staff in his hand he spent the whole night. He left at daybreak so as not to be recognized. He did not take the road that led straight to Barcelona, where he would encounter many who would recognize and honor him, but he went off to a town called Manresa. There he decided to stay in a hospice a few days and also to note some things in his book that he carefully carried with him and by which he was greatly consoled. After he had gone about a league from Montserrat, a man who had been hurrying after him caught up to him and asked if he had given some clothing to a poor man, as the poor man said. Answering that he had, the tears ran from his eyes in compassion for the poor man to whom he had given the clothes—in compassion, for he realized they were threatening him, thinking he had stolen them. Yet as much as he avoided esteem, he could not remain long in Manresa before people were saying great things, as the story of what happened at Montserrat spread. Eventu-ally they said more than the truth, that he had given up much wealth and so forth.

4. Ignatius's confessor was the French priest Jean Chanon. He was a monk of the Benedictine abbey of Montserrat and a man noted for his intense and austere spiritual-ity. He introduced Ignatius to the *Ejercitatorio de la vida espiritual*, a work composed by Montserrat's previous abbot and reformer, Garcia Ximenes de Cisneros, and in the tradition of the *Devotio moderna*. See Leturia, *Iñigo de Loyola*, pp. 148 ff.; and Evennett, *Counter-Reformation*, pp. 58–9.

CHAPTER 3

Manresa
(March 1522–Early 1523)

Each day he begged alms in Manresa. He did not eat meat or drink wine, even though they were offered to him. He did not fast on Sundays, and if they gave him a little wine, he drank it. As he had been very attentive in taking care of his hair, as was the fashion at that time (and he had a fine head of hair), he decided to let it grow naturally, without combing or cutting it or covering it with anything by night or day. For the same reason he let his toenails and fingernails grow because he also had been attentive to this. While in this hospice it often happened that on a bright day he could see something in the air near him; because it was indeed very beautiful, it gave him great comfort. He could not discern very well the kind of thing it was, but in a way it seemed to him to have the form of a serpent with many things that shone like eyes, though they were not eyes. He found great pleasure and consolation in seeing this thing, and the more he saw it the more his consolation increased. When it disappeared he was saddened.

Until this time he had remained always in nearly the same interior state of great and steady happiness, without having any knowledge of the inward things of the spirit. During those days while the vision lasted or somewhat before it began (for it lasted many days), a harsh thought came to trouble him by pointing out the hardship of his life, as if some one was saying within his soul, "How will you be able to endure this life for the seventy years you have yet to live?" Believing that the thought came from the enemy, he answered inwardly with great vehemence, "O miserable being! Can you promise me an hour of life?" So he overcame the temptation and remained at peace. This was the first temptation that came to him after the affair mentioned above. It happened when he was entering a church where he heard solemn mass each day and Vespers and Compline which were sung entirely and gave him great consolation. Usually he read the passion at mass, always retaining his equanimity.

But soon after the temptation noted above he began to experience great changes in his soul. Sometimes he found himself so disagreeable that he took no joy in prayer or in hearing mass or in any other prayer he said. At other times exactly the opposite of this came over him so suddenly that he seemed to have thrown off sadness and desolation just as one snatches a cape from another's shoulders. Here he began to be astounded by these changes that he had never experienced before, and he said to himself, "What new life is this that we are now beginning?" At this time he still conversed occasionally with spiritual persons who had faith in him and wanted to talk to him, because, even though he had no knowledge of spiritual matters, yet in his speech he revealed great fervor and willingness to go forward in God's service. At that time there was at Manresa a woman of great age who had long been a servant of God and who was known as such in many parts of Spain, so much so that the Catholic king had summoned her once to tell her something. One day this woman, speaking to the new soldier of Christ, said to him, "O! May my Lord Jesus Christ deign to appear to you someday." But he was amazed at this, taking the matter literally, "How would Jesus Christ appear to me?" He persevered continually in his usual confession and communion each Sunday.

But he began to have many difficulties about this from scruples, for even though the general confession he had made at Montserrat had been made with enough care and had been completely written, as has been said, still at times it seemed to him that he had not confessed certain things. This caused him much distress, because although he confessed it, he was not satisfied. Thus he began to look for some spiritual men who could cure him of these scruples, but nothing helped him. At last a very spiritual man, a doctor of the cathedral who preached there, told him one day in confession to write down everything he could remember. He did so, but after confession the scruples still returned and each time in more detail so that he was very troubled. Although he realized that those scruples did him much harm and that it would be wise to be rid of them, he could not do that himself. Sometimes he thought it might cure him if his confessor would order him in the name of Jesus Christ not to confess anything from the past; he wanted his confessor to direct him thus, but he did not dare say so to his confessor.

But without his saying so, his confessor ordered him not to confess anything from the past, unless it should be something very clear. But inasmuch as he thought all those things were very clear, this order was of no benefit to him, and so he continued with his difficulty. At this time he was staying in a small room that the Dominicans had given him in their monastery. He persevered in his seven hours of prayer on his knees, getting up continually at midnight and doing all the other exercises already mentioned. But he found no cure for his scruples in any of them; many months had now passed since they had begun to torment him. Once when he was very upset by them he began to pray with such fervor that he shouted out loud to God, saying, "Help me, Lord, for I find no remedy among men nor in any creature, yet if I thought I could find it, no labor would be too great for me. Show me, O Lord, where I may find it; even though I should have to follow a little dog so he could help me, I would do it."

While he had these thoughts, the temptation often came over him with great force to throw himself into a large hole in his room next to the place where he was praying. But realizing that it was a sin to kill oneself, he shouted again, "Lord, I will do nothing to offend you," repeating these words many times, as well as the previous ones. Then there came to his mind the story of a saint who, in order to obtain something from God that he wanted very much, went without eating many days until he got it. Thinking about this for a good while, he at last decided to do it, telling himself that he would not eat or drink until God took care of him or until he saw that death was indeed near; for if he saw that he was at that point where he would have to die if he did not eat, then he would decide to ask for bread and to eat (as if at that point he could in fact ask·for it or eat it).

This happened one Sunday after he had received communion; he persevered the whole week without putting anything into his mouth nor ceasing to do his usual exercises, even going to divine office and saying his prayers on his knees, even at midnight and so forth. But when the next Sunday came and he had to go to confession, because he used to tell his confessor in very great detail what he had done, he also told him how he had eaten nothing during that week. His confessor ordered him to break off his abstinence; though he still felt strong he obeyed his confessor and that day and the next felt free from scruples. But on the third day, which was Tuesday, while at prayer he began to remember his sins one by one, and he went on thinking about one sin after the other out of his past and felt he was required to confess them again. But after these thoughts, disgust for the life he led and the desire to give it up came over him. In this way the Lord wished to awaken him as if from a dream. From the lessons God had given him he now had some experience of the diversity of spirits, and he began to wonder about the means by which that spirit had come. He decided very clearly, therefore, not to confess anything from the past anymore; from that day forward he remained free of those scruples and held it for certain that Our Lord through his mercy had wished to deliver him.

Besides his seven hours of prayer he busied himself by helping certain souls in spiritual matters, who came there looking for him. All the rest of the day he spent thinking about the things of God that he had meditated upon or read about that day.[1] But when he went

1. One of the books Ignatius read at Manresa was Thomas à Kempis's *Imitation of Christ,* and it became thereafter a book of devotion he especially favored, recommended, and constantly read. Câmara reports this not in the autobiography but in his

to bed great enlightenment, great spiritual consolations often came
to him, so that he lost much of the time he had intended for sleeping,
which was not much. Wondering about this at times he thought to
himself that he had assigned much time for converse with God and
all the rest of the day as well, and he began to doubt, therefore,
whether that enlightenment came from a good spirit; he concluded
that it would be better to ignore it and to sleep for the appointed
time. And so he did.

He continued to abstain from eating meat and was so firm about
it that he would not think of changing it for any reason; but one
morning after he arose some meat appeared before him, as if he saw
it with his eyes, though he had not had any desire for it. At the same
time he also had a strong inclination of his will to eat it from that
time on. Although he remembered his previous intention, he could
not hesitate about this and decided that he ought to eat meat. Later,
when telling this to his confessor, the confessor told him to consider
whether perhaps this was a temptation; but examining it carefully,
he could never be in doubt about it.

God treated him at this time just as a schoolmaster treats a child
whom he is teaching. Whether this was on account of his coarseness
or his dense intelligence or because he had no one to teach him or
because of the strong desire God himself had given him to serve
Him, he clearly believed and has always believed that God treated
him in this way. Indeed if he were to doubt this, he thought he would
offend His divine majesty. Something of this can be seen from the
five following points.

FIRST. He had great devotion to the Most Holy Trinity,
and each day he said a prayer to the three Persons individually.
But as he also said a prayer to the Most Holy Trinity the thought
came to him: why did he say four prayers to the Trinity? But this
thought, as something of small importance, gave him little or no
difficulty. One day while saying the Hours of Our Lady on the

steps of the monastery itself, his understanding began to be elevated so that he saw the Most Holy Trinity in the form of three keys.[2] This brought on so many tears and so much sobbing that he could not control himself. While going in a procession that set out from there that morning, he could not hold back his tears until dinnertime; after eating he could not stop talking about the Most Holy Trinity, using many different comparisons and with great joy and consolation. As a result the impression of experiencing great devotion while praying to the Most Holy Trinity has remained with him throughout his life.

SECOND. One time the manner in which God had created the world was revealed to his understanding with great spiritual joy. He seemed to see something white, from which some rays were coming, and God made light from this. But he did not know how to explain these things, nor did he remember very well the spiritual enlightenment that God was impressing on his soul at that time.

THIRD. At Mànresa, too, where he stayed almost a year, after God began to comfort him and he saw the fruit which He brought forth in treating souls, he gave up those extremes he had formerly observed, and he now cut his nails and his hair. One day in this town while he was hearing mass in the church of the monastery mentioned above, at the elevation of the Body of the Lord, he saw with interior eyes something like white rays coming from above. Although he cannot explain this very well after so long a time, nevertheless what he saw clearly with his understanding was how Jesus Christ our Lord was there in that most holy sacrament.

FOURTH. Often and for a long time, while at prayer, he saw with interior eyes the humanity of Christ. The form that appeared

2. This image or figure of the Trinity refers to the keys—*teclas*—of a musical instrument and probably signifies a musical chord—three notes producing a single harmony. According to Hugo Rahner this vision marks the end of Ignatius's "night of the soul" and the beginning of the divine enlightenment that occurs at Manresa. Rahner, *Spirituality of St. Ignatius Loyola,* p. 50.

to him was like a white body, neither very large nor very small, but he did not see the members distinctly. He saw this at Manresa many times. If he should say twenty or forty, he would not be so bold as to say it was a lie. He saw it another time at Jerusalem and still another while traveling near Padua. He has also seen our Lady in a similar form, without distinguishing parts. The things he saw strengthened him then and always gave him such strength in his faith that he often thought to himself: if there were no Scriptures to teach us these matters of the faith, he would be resolved to die for them, only because of what he had seen.[3]

FIFTH. One time he was going out of his devotion to a church a little more than a mile from Manresa; I believe it was called St. Paul's. The road ran next to the river. As he went along occupied with his devotions, he sat down for a little while with his face toward the river which was running deep. While he was seated there, the eyes of his understanding began to be opened; though he did not see any vision, he understood and knew many things, both spiritual things and matters of faith and of learning, and this was with so great an enlightenment that everything seemed new to him.[4] Though there were many, he cannot set forth the details that he understood then, except that he experienced a great clarity in his understanding. This was such that in the whole course of his life, through sixty-two years, even if he

3. Joseph de Guibert, S.J., in his masterful work on Ignatian and Jesuit spirituality, *The Jesuits, Their Spiritual Doctrine and Practice,* trans. William J. Young, S.J. (Chicago, 1964), pp. 31–32, comments on the contrast between the importance and content of these inward visions that Ignatius experienced and so long remembered and the great poverty of their imaginative element. He sees these visions as essentially intellectual, their images reflecting or signifying Ignatius's spiritual enlightenment but not constituting or communicating it.

4. This mystical experience or "illumination" on the banks of the river Cardoner near Manresa has always been viewed as a decisive moment in the life of Ignatius. There are different explanations of its content or substance, but it is obvious that Ignatius gained, or believed he gained, at this moment a broader and deeper understanding of his faith and his vocation. The most characteristic features of Ignatius's spirituality and apostolate are generally associated with it. See Rahner, *Spirituality of St. Ignatius Loyola,* pp. 51ff; and Leonardo R. Silos, S.J., "Cardoner in the Life of Saint Ignatius of Loyola," *Archivum Historicum Societatis Iesu* 33 (1964): 3–43.

gathered up all the many helps he had had from God and all the many things he knew and added them together, he does not think they would amount to as much as he had received at that one time.

After this had lasted for a good while, he went to kneel before a nearby cross to give thanks to God. There, the vision that had appeared to him many times but which he had never understood, that is, the thing mentioned above which seemed very beautiful to him and had many eyes, now appeared to him. But while kneeling before the cross, he saw clearly that the object did not have its usual beautiful color, and with a strong affirmation of his will he knew very clearly that it came from the demon. For a long time after it often appeared to him, but as a sign of contempt he drove it away with a staff he used to carry in his hand.

Once while he was ill at Manresa a very severe fever brought him to death's door, and he fully believed that his soul was about to leave him. At this a thought came to him telling him that he was just, but this caused him so much trouble that he rejected it and recalled his sins to mind. He had more trouble with this thought than with the fever itself, but no matter how much he strove to overcome the thought, he could not do so. Somewhat relieved of the fever so that he was not at the point of expiring, he began to cry out loudly, calling him a sinner and reminding him of the offenses he had committed against God.

Another time while going from Valencia to Italy by sea, the rudder of the ship was broken in a terrible storm, and the situation reached such a point that in his judgment and that of many others who sailed on the ship, they could not by natural means escape death. At this time, examining himself carefully and preparing to die, he was unable to be afraid of his sins or of being condemned, but he was greatly confused and sorrowful, as he believed he had not well used the gifts and graces which God our Lord had given him.

Another time, in the year 1550, he was very ill with a very severe sickness which, in his opinion and that of many others, would be his last. At this time, thinking about death, he felt such happiness and such spiritual consolation at having to die that he dissolved entirely into tears. This happened so continually that he often stopped thinking about death so as not to feel so much consolation.

When winter [1522] came he fell ill with a very severe sickness, and for his care the city put him in a house belonging to the father of one Ferrera, who was later in the service of Baltasar de Faria.[5] There he was treated with great attention, and many prominent ladies, out of affection for him, came to watch over him by night.[6] Though he recovered from this sickness, he was still very weak and frequently suffered stomach pains. For these reasons, therefore, and because the winter was very cold, they made him dress better and wear shoes and cover his head; they made him wear two brown doublets of very coarse cloth and a bonnet of the same stuff, a kind of beret. At this time there were many days when he was anxious to talk about spiritual matters and to find persons who could do so. Meanwhile, the time when he planned to set out for Jerusalem was approaching.

At the beginning of the year 1523 he set out for Barcelona to take ship. Although various people offered to accompany him, he wanted to go alone, for his whole purpose was to have God alone as his refuge. One day when some people were insisting that, because he didn't know either the Italian or Latin languages, he ought to have a companion, telling him how much this would help him and strongly urging it upon him, he said that he would not go even in the company of the son or the brother of the duke of Cardona, because he wanted to practice three virtues—charity, faith, and hope. If he took a companion, he would expect help from him when

5. Baltasar de Faria was a business agent at Rome for the Portuguese king from 1543 to 1551. Ignatius undoubtedly had many contacts with him, John III of Portugal being a great patron of the Society.

6. Among the ladies who befriended Ignatius at Manresa was the widow Inés Pascual whom he had met as he was coming down from Montserrat toward Manresa. They became close and life-long friends, and Ignatius's first extant letter (1524) is a letter of spiritual advice addressed to her. On her and other "prominent ladies" Ignatius knew at Manresa and Barcelona, see Hugo Rahner, S.J., *Saint Ignatius Loyola, Letters to Women* (New York, 1960), pp. 173–84.

he was hungry; if he fell down, he would expect him to help him get up; and he would also confide in him and would feel affection for him on this account; but he wanted to place that confidence, affection, and hope in God alone. What he said in this way, he felt in his heart. With these thoughts, he not only had the desire to set out alone but to go without any provisions. When he began to arrange for his passage, he persuaded the master of the ship to carry him free, as he had no money, but on condition that he brought to the ship some biscuit to sustain himself; in no other way in the world would they take him aboard.

Great scruples came over him (so strongly as to cause him great trouble) when he went to obtain the biscuit. "Is this the hope and faith you have in God who would not fail you?" and so forth. At last, not knowing what to do because he saw probable reasons on both sides, he decided to place himself in the hands of his confessor. He told him how much he wanted to seek perfection and to do whatever would be more to the glory of God and the reasons that had caused him to question whether he ought to take any sustenance. The confessor said that he should beg for what was necessary and take it with him. When he begged from a lady, she asked where he wanted to go. He hesitated a bit whether he would tell her, but at last he resolved to say no more than that he was going to Italy and to Rome. Surprised, she said, "Do you want to go to Rome? Well, I don't know how those who go there come back." (By this she meant that in Rome they profited little from the things of the spirit.)[7] The reason why he didn't dare say that he was going to Jerusalem was for fear of vainglory. This fear disturbed him so much that he never dared say from what country he came or to what family he belonged. At least, having obtained the biscuit, he went on board. Standing on the shore he found that he had five or six *blancas,* given him when he was begging from door to door (for he used to live that way); he left them on a bench that he found near the shore.

---

7. This lady (Rahner suggests) may have been the noble lady Isabel Roser whom Ignatius met in Barcelona at this time and who became a close friend and benefactress. Ibid., pp. 262–63. See also Appendix I.

After being in Barcelona a little more than twenty days, he embarked. While he was still in Barcelona before setting sail, as was his custom he sought out spiritual persons for conversation, even though they lived in hermitages far from the city. But neither in Barcelona nor in Manresa during the whole time he was there did he find persons who could help him as much as he wished; only in Manresa that woman, who was mentioned above, who told him to ask God that Jesus Christ might appear to him. She alone seemed to him to enter more deeply into spiritual matters. Therefore, after leaving Barcelona, he completely lost this eagerness to seek out spiritual persons.

Ignatius boarding a ship at Barcelona to begin his voyage to the Holy Land.

CHAPTER 4

The Journey to Jerusalem
(March–September 1523)

They had such a strong wind at the stern that they reached Gaeta from Barcelona in five days and nights, though they were all very frightened because of the great storm.[1] Throughout all that region there was fear of pestilence, but as soon as he disembarked he began the journey to Rome. A mother and her daughter, who wore boy's clothing, and another young man, who had come on the ship, accompanied him. They went with him because they also were begging. When they arrived at a hostel they found around a great fire many soldiers who gave them something to eat and a good deal of wine, urging them on as if they wanted to warm them up. Later they were separated, the mother and daughter being lodged in a room upstairs and the pilgrim and the young man in the stable. But at midnight he heard loud cries coming from above; getting up to see what it was, he found the mother and her daughter full of tears in the courtyard below, wailing that they had attempted to rape them. At this such a strong feeling came over him that he began to shout, "Does this have to be endured?" and similar protests. He said this with such energy that all those in the house were astonished, so much

1. Gaeta is due east of Barcelona, on the Italian coast about seventy-five miles south of Rome.

so that no one did him any harm. The young man had already fled, and, though it was still night, all three began their journey.

When they arrived at a nearby city, they found it closed. Unable to enter, the three of them spent the night in a damp church there. In the morning the city was closed to them, and they found no alms outside, even though they went to a castle which seemed nearby. There the pilgrim felt weak because of the hardship of the sea voyage as well as of other trials, and, unable to travel farther, he remained there. But the mother and her daughter went on to Rome. That day many people came out of the city; learning that the lady of the land had come out, he went to her and told her that he was ill only from weakness and asked her to let him enter the city to seek a remedy. She readily granted it, and he began to beg in the city and obtained many *quatrini* [small coins]. After resting there two days, he set out on his journey again and arrived at Rome on Palm Sunday.

There all who spoke to him, on discovering that he didn't carry any money for Jerusalem, began to dissuade him from making that trip, giving him many reasons why it was impossible to find passage without money. But he had great assurance in his soul (which he couldn't doubt) that he would find a way to go to Jerusalem. After receiving the blessing of Pope Adrian VI, he then set out for Venice eight or nine days after Easter.[2] He had six or seven ducats which they had given him for the passage from Venice to Jerusalem; he had accepted them, being somewhat overcome by the fears they had aroused that he would not be able to go in any other way. But two days after leaving Rome he began to realize that this was a lack of trust on his part, and it bothered him a good deal that he had accepted the ducats, so he decided it would be good to get rid of them. He finally decided to give them freely to those whom he

2. It was customary for the pilgrim who was Jerusalem bound to go to Rome to receive permission and the papal blessing for his pilgrimage. Adrian VI had been elected pope in January 1522 while he was in Spain, where he served as regent for King Charles, now Emperor Charles V, and had preceded Ignatius to Rome the previous summer. Their respective journeys across northern Spain to Catalonia almost coincided.

encountered, who usually were poor. He did so, and when he arrived at Venice, he had no more than a few *quatrini* which he needed that night.

While on the journey to Venice he slept in doorways because of the guards set against the pestilence. It happened once that when he got up in the morning he collided with a man, who, seeing what he saw, fled in great fear because he must have seemed very pale to him. Traveling in this way, he came to Chioggia with some companions who had joined him; he learned that they would not be allowed to enter Venice. As his companions decided to go to Padua to obtain a certificate of health there, he set out with them. But he couldn't travel very well, and they went on very rapidly leaving him at nightfall in a large field. While he was there Christ appeared to him in the manner in which He usually appeared to him, as we have mentioned above,[3] and this comforted him very much. Consoled in this way, the next morning, without forging a certificate as I believe his companions had done, he came to the gates of Padua and entered without the guards asking anything of him. The same thing happened when he left. This greatly astonished his companions who came to obtain a certificate so they could go to Venice, though he didn't concern himself about it.

When they arrived at Venice, the guards came to the boat to examine everyone, one by one, as many as there were, but they left him alone. He sustained himself in Venice by begging, and he slept in St. Mark's square. He had no wish to go to the house of the emperor's ambassador, nor did he take any special care to seek the wherewithal for his passage. He had a great certainty in his soul that God would give him the means to go to Jerusalem; this strengthened him so much that no arguments or fears suggested to him could cause him to doubt. One day he met a rich Spaniard who asked him what he was doing and where he wanted to go. Learning his purpose, he took him home to eat and kept him there a few days until his departure was arranged. Ever since Manresa the pilgrim had the

3. See pp. 38–9.

habit when he ate with anyone not to speak at the table except to answer briefly; but he listened to what was said and noted some things which he took as the occasion to speak about God, and when the meal was finished, he did so.

This was the reason why the good man and all his household were so fond of him and wanted him to stay and tried to keep him there. The host himself brought him to the doge of Venice so he could speak to him, that is, he obtained entrance and an audience for him. When the doge heard the pilgrim, he ordered that he be given passage on the ship of the governors who were going to Cyprus. Although many pilgrims had come that year to go to Jerusalem, most of them had returned to their own countries because of the recent event which had occurred, the fall of Rhodes. Even so there were thirteen in the pilgrim ship which sailed first, and eight or nine remained for the governors' ship.[4] While he was awaiting departure, a high fever came over our pilgrim, but, after treating him badly a few days, it left him. The ship sailed on the day he took a purge. The people of the house asked the doctor if he could embark for Jerusalem, and the doctor said that indeed he could embark, if he wanted to be buried there. He embarked and sailed that day. He vomited a good bit and felt relieved and began to recover completely.

He severely condemned some obscenities and indecencies that were done openly on the ship. The Spaniards who were there warned him not to do so, because the ship's crew were planning to leave him on some island. But our Lord willed that they should arrive quickly at Cyprus. Leaving the ship there [Famagusta] they went overland to another port called Las Salinas [Larnaca], ten

4. In addition to Ignatius's rather sparse account of this journey, there are the more detailed diaries of two of his fellow pilgrims, Peter Füssli of Zurich and Philip Hagen of Strasbourg. Füssli traveled on the so-called governers' ship with Ignatius and informs us there were four Spanish pilgrims aboard including Diego Manes, whom Ignatius mentions below. Hagen was on the pilgrim ship. Both vessels came to Cyprus, but only the pilgrim ship, carrying all the pilgrims, made the passage across to the Holy Land. For further details, see James Brodrick, S.J., *Saint Ignatius Loyola, The Pilgrim Years* (New York, 1956), pp. 129ff; or Paul Dudon, S.J., *St. Ignatius of Loyola*, trans. William J. Young, S.J. (Milwaukee, 1949), pp. 78ff.

leagues from there. They boarded the pilgrim ship, but he brought no more for his sustenance than his hope in God, as he had done on the other ship. During all this time our Lord appeared to him many times, giving him great consolation and strength. It seemed to him that he saw something round and large, as though it were gold, and this appeared to him after they left Cyprus until they arrived at Jaffa. As they were journeying to Jerusalem on little donkeys, as was the custom, a Spaniard, a noble it would seem named Diego Manes, two miles before reaching Jerusalem suggested with great devotion to all the pilgrims that since in a little while they would reach the place from which they could see the Holy City, it would be good for all to prepare their consciences and go in silence.

This seemed good to them all, and each one began to recollect himself. A little bit before coming to the place from where they would see [the city], they dismounted, because they saw the friars with a cross who were waiting for them. On seeing the city the pilgrim felt great consolation which was common to them all, as the others said, and a joy which did not seem natural. He always felt the same devotion on his visits to the holy places. His firm intention was to remain in Jerusalem continually visiting the holy places, and, in addition to this devotion, he also planned to help souls. For this reason he brought letters of recommendation for the guardian and gave them to him.[5] He also told him of his intention to remain there because of his devotion but not the second part about wanting to help souls, because he had not told this to anyone, though he had frequently spoken about the first part. The guardian answered that he did not see how he could stay because the house was in such need that it could not support the friars; for that reason he had decided to send some back to these parts [that is, Europe] with the pilgrims. The pilgrim replied that he wanted nothing from the house, except only that when he came at times to confess, they would hear his

5. The holy places were in the care of the Franciscans. A guardian is the head or superior of a Franciscan monastery, and the guardian here referred to was probably the friar in charge of the monastery of Mount Sion in Jerusalem.

confession. With that the guardian told him that he could do that but that he would have to wait until the provincial (I believe he was the head of the order in that area), who was at Bethlehem, returned.

Assured by this promise, the pilgrim began to write letters to Barcelona to spiritual persons. Having already written one and while writing another on the eve of the departure of the pilgrims, he was summoned by the provincial (who had returned) and the guardian. The provincial told him kindly that he knew of his good intention to remain in the holy places and he had given much thought to the matter, but because of the experience he had had with others, he decided that it would not be wise. Many had had that desire, but some had been captured and others killed and the order had later been obliged to ransom the captives. Therefore he should prepare to leave the next day with the pilgrims. He replied that he was very firm in his purpose and had resolved that he would not fail to carry it out for any reason. He frankly gave the provincial to understand that, even though he did not approve, he would not abandon his intention out of any fear, unless it was a matter on which he could compel him under pain of sin. To this the provincial replied that they had authority from the Apostolic See to compel anyone whom they wished to leave or to remain there and to excommunicate anyone who did not wish to obey them and that in this matter they were determined that he should not remain, and so forth.

He wanted to show him the bulls giving them power to excommunicate, but he said he didn't need to see them, as he believed their reverences; inasmuch as they had decided with the authority they had, he would obey them. When this was over he returned to where he had been before. Since it was not Our Lord's will that he remain in those holy places, he felt a strong desire to visit Mount Olivet again before leaving. On Mount Olivet there is a stone from which Our Lord rose up to heaven, and His footprints are still seen there; this was what he wanted to see again. So without saying anything or taking a guide (for those who go without a Turk as guide run a great risk), he stole away from the others and went alone to Mount Olivet. But the guards did not want to let him enter. He gave them a desk knife that he carried, and after saying his prayer with deep consolation he felt the desire to go to Bethphage. While there he remembered that he had not clearly noticed on Mount Olivet in what direction the right foot was pointed nor in what direction the left. Returning there, I believe he gave his scissors to the guards so they would let him enter.

When it was learned in the monastery that he had gone out without a guide, the friars took steps to find him. So as he was coming down from Mount Olivet he met a "Christian of the belt" that is, a Syrian Christian who served in the monastery. He had a large staff and with a great show of annoyance made signs of striking him. When he came up to him he grabbed him harshly by the arm, but he let himself be led easily. The good man, however, never let him go. As he went along the road held in this way by the "Christian of the belt," he felt great consolation from our Lord, and it seemed to him that he saw Christ over him continually. This [consolation] lasted in great abundance until they reached the monastery.

Barcinone vt se ad animorum salutem instruat
prima Grammaticæ elementa annos tres. et tri =
ginta natus addiscit; furente ac rumpente se
Dæmone, qui importunus rerum cælestium gau =
dijs auocare alio eius animum frustra conatur.

32

Ignatius as a student in Barcelona.

CHAPTER 5

The Return to Spain (September 1523–Early 1524)

The next day they set out, and after arriving at Cyprus, the pilgrims went off in different ships. There were in the port three or four ships bound for Venice. One was a Turkish ship, another was a very small boat, and the third was a very rich and powerful ship belonging to a rich Venetian. Some pilgrims asked the master of this ship if he would take the pilgrim, but when he learned that he had no money, he did not want to, even though many people asked him and praised the pilgrim, and so forth. The master answered that if he were a saint, he could travel as St. James had done or something like that.[1] These petitioners very easily obtained their request from the master of the small ship. They set out one day in the morning with a good wind; but in the afternoon a storm came upon them, and the ships were scattered. The great ship was lost near the islands of Cyprus, and only the people escaped; in the same storm the Turkish ship was lost and all the people on it. The small ship suffered much difficulty, but in the end they landed in Apulia. This was in the dead of winter, and it was very cold and snowing. The pilgrim had no clothing other

1. According to the legend, the body of St. James was miraculously transported on a ship divinely provided from the Holy Land to a port on the northwest coast of Spain, whence originated the great shrine of Santiago de Compostela.

than some breeches of coarse cloth reaching the knee, but his legs were bare; he had shoes and a jacket of black cloth, opened by many slashes at the shoulders, and a short doublet of thin hair.

He arrived at Venice in mid-January in the year 1524, having been at sea from Cyprus the whole months of November and December and the first half of January. In Venice one of the two men who had received him in his house before he set out for Jerusalem met him and gave him as alms fifteen or sixteen *giulii* and a piece of cloth, which he folded many times and put over his stomach because of the great cold. After the pilgrim realized that it was not God's will that he remain in Jerusalem, he continually pondered within himself what he ought to do. At last he inclined more to study for some time so he would be able to help souls, and he decided to go to Barcelona. So he set out from Venice for Genoa. One day in Ferrara in the principal church at his devotions, a poor man asked him for alms and he gave him a *marchetto,* which is a coin of five or six *quatrini.* After that another man came, and he gave him another small coin that he had, somewhat greater [in value], and to a third man he gave a *giulio,* as he had nothing but *giulii.* The poor people, seeing that he was giving alms, kept coming until he had given away everything he had. Finally, many poor people came together to ask alms. He asked them to pardon him as he had nothing more.

Thus he left Ferrara for Genoa. On the road he met some Spanish soldiers who treated him well that night, but they were very much amazed that he traveled by that road, because it was necessary to pass almost through the middle of both armies, the French and the imperial.[2] They asked him to leave the royal road and to take another safer one that they pointed out to him. But he did not take their advice. Instead, traveling on the main road he came upon a burned and destroyed village, and until nighttime he found no one to give him anything to eat. But when the sun went down he came to a

2. Ignatius was crossing a region where the French and the Spanish imperial armies of Charles V were maneuvering and struggling for possession of the duchy of Milan. This was an important phase of a conflict that lasted through the decade of the 1520s (and beyond) and in which Ignatius himself had played a part in 1521 at Pamplona.

walled place where the guards immediately seized him, thinking he was a spy. They put him in a small house next to the gate and began to question him, as is usual when there is some suspicion, but he replied to all their questions that he knew nothing. They stripped him and searched him down to his shoes and all the parts of his body to see if he was carrying any letters. Unable to learn anything by any means, they bound him to take him to the captain, who would make him talk. He asked them to take him clothed in his doublet, but they refused to give it to him and took him in his breeches and jacket mentioned above.

On the way the pilgrim saw a kind of representation of Christ being led away, but this was not a vision like the others. He was taken through three main streets, and he went without any sadness, but rather with joy and contentment. It was his custom to speak to any person, no matter who he might be, using the familiar "you" [vos], observing this devotion because Christ and the apostles had spoken in this way and so forth. As he was going through the streets, the thought came to mind, together with fear of the tortures they would inflict on him, that it would be wise to give up that custom in this situation and to speak formally [por señoria] to the captain, and so forth. But then he recognized that this was a temptation. Since it is such, he said, I will not speak formally to him nor will I show him reverence nor will I take off my cap.

They reached the captain's palace and left him in a lower room. A while later the captain spoke to him. Without showing any form of courtesy, he answered in a few words with a noticeable space between one word and the next. The captain took him for a madman and said so to those who had brought him; "This man is out of his senses. Give him his things and throw him out." Leaving the palace he then met a Spaniard who lived there; he took him to his house and gave him something to break his fast and all the necessities for that night. Setting out in the morning, he traveled until evening when two soldiers in a tower saw him and came down to seize him. They took him to their captain, who was French; the captain asked him, among other things, from what country he came, and learning that he was from Guipúzcoa, he said to him, "I come from near there," apparently from near Bayonne.[3] Then he said, "Take him and give him something to eat and treat him well." On this road from Ferrara to Genoa many other trivial things happened. At last he reached Genoa where a Vizcayan named Portundo, who had spoken with him on other occasions when he served in the court of the Catholic king, recognized him. This man got him passage on a ship going to Barcelona, which ran great danger of being captured by Andrea Doria, who was then in the French service and gave pursuit to it.[4]

3. Bayonne is in France across the border from the Spanish province of Guipúzcoa. It is all Basque country, and the French captain, it appears, was a Basque like Ignatius.

4. Andrea Doria was the famous Genoese admiral. Although Genoa was on the side of Charles V in the war then going on (hence Ignatius could embark for Barcelona), Doria himself, fearing the subjection of his country, joined the French. He later switched to the emperor's side and served him notably for many years.

Compluti primum; postea Salmanticæ, calumnias
pro Christo, et carcerem passus, ex ipso etiam car-
cere animas lucratur, magnoq spiritus feruore
succensus. Non tot inquit in hac vrbe sunt com-
pedes, quin plures ego Christi causa percupiam.

30

Ignatius imprisoned at Alcalá.

CHAPTER 6

Studies at Barcelona and Alcalá
(Lent 1524–June 1527)

When he arrived at Barcelona he made known his wish to study to Isabel Roser and to a Master Ardévol who taught grammar.[1] To both this seemed very wise; he [Ardévol] offered to teach him for nothing, and she offered to give him what he needed to support himself. In Manresa the pilgrim had met a friar (of the order of St. Bernard, I think), a very spiritual man; he wanted to stay with him to learn and to be able to give himself more easily to the spirit and also to be of help to souls. So he replied that he would accept the offer if he did not find the opportunity he was looking for at Manresa. But when he went there he found that the friar was dead, and so, returning to Barcelona, he began to study with great diligence. But one thing distressed him a good deal, and that was when he began to memorize, as is necessary at the beginning of grammar, new understanding of spiritual things and new pleasures came to him in such a way that he could not memorize, nor could he drive them away no matter how much he tried.

1. On Isabel Roser, see Chapter 3, note 7 and Rahner, *Saint Ignatius Loyola, Letters to Women,* pp. 262–95. Ardévol taught Latin grammar in the University of Barcelona, though the picture has come down of Ignatius in his thirties seated with the small boys of Ardévol's class, learning his declensions and conjugations. During these years in Barcelona, Ignatius stayed in the home of Inés Pascual, sharing a room with her son Juan. See Chapter 3, note 6 and ibid., pp. 173–84.

So, thinking often about this, he said to himself, "Not even when I go to pray nor when I am at mass do such vivid insights come to me." Thus, little by little, he came to realize that this was a temptation. After saying a prayer he went to Santa Maria del Mar, near the master's house, as he had asked him to please listen to him a while in that church. Thus, when they were seated, he told him faithfully everything that occurred in his soul and what little progress he had made until then for that reason; but he promised his master, saying, "I promise you never to fail to hear your lessons these two years, so long as I can find bread and water in Barcelona to support myself." As he made this promise with great emphasis, he never again had those temptations. The stomach pain which he had suffered at Manresa, for which reason he wore shoes, left him, and his stomach felt as well as it had after he set out for Jerusalem. For this reason, while he was studying at Barcelona, he felt the desire to resume his previous penances and so he began to make a hole in the soles of his shoes. He continued to widen it little by little so that when the winter cold came, he had only the upper part of his shoes.

After two years of study in which, as they told him, he had made great progress, his master informed him he could now study the liberal arts and should go to Alcalá.[2] But still he had a doctor of theology examine him, and he gave him the same advice. So he set out alone for Alcalá, although I believe he already had some companions.[3] When he arrived at Alcalá, he began to beg and to live on alms. After he lived in this fashion for ten or twelve days, a cleric and others who were with him, seeing him beg alms one day, began to laugh at him and to say insulting things to him, as one usually does

2. A new University had been established at Alcalá de Henares in 1508 by the great primate of Spain, Cardinal Ximenes de Cisneros, for the education of the clergy. Though it had the traditional courses in the arts and theology, with chairs for Thomism, Scotism, and nominalism, it was also the center of humanism in Spain. Its original college of San Ildefonso was the first trilingual college in Europe. The famous Complutensian polyglot Bible also was published in Alcalá just a few years before Ignatius's arrival.

3. Ignatius will say more about these companions—Calixto de Sa, Juan de Arteaga, and Lope de Cáceres—who soon followed him to Alcalá, as he progresses in the autobiography.

to those who, though they may be healthy, go begging. At this moment the man who had charge of the new hospital of Antezana passed by and, taking pity on him, called him and took him to the hospital where he gave him a room and all he needed.

He studied at Alcalá almost a year and a half. Because he arrived at Barcelona in Lent in the year 1524 and studied there for two years, he arrived at Alcalá in the year 1526. He studied the logic of Soto, the physics of Albert, and the Master of the Sentences.[4] While at Alcalá he was busy giving spiritual exercises and teaching Christian doctrine and in so doing brought forth fruit for the glory of God. There were many persons who came to a full knowledge and delight in spiritual things; but others had various temptations, such as the one who wanted to scourge himself but could not do so, as though someone was holding back his hand, and other similar cases. These gave rise to rumors among the people, especially because of the great crowd that gathered wherever he was teaching doctrine. Soon after he arrived at Alcalá, he became acquainted with Don Diego de Eguía who lived in the house of his brother who had a printing shop in Alcalá and was well-to-do.[5] They helped him with alms to support the poor and kept the pilgrim's three companions in their house. Once when he came to ask alms for some necessities, Don Diego told him that he had no money, but he opened a chest

4. Domingo de Soto (1494–1560) was one of the renowned Thomist theologians at Salamanca in the sixteenth century. Some early version of his work in logic was evidently studied at Alcalá at this time. Albert the Great, a thirteenth-century philosopher-theologian and preceptor of St. Thomas Aquinas, wrote an extensive commentary on Aristotle's physics. The Master of the Sentences is Peter Lombard, a twelfth-century theologian whose work *Sententiarum libri quatuor* was the basis for all advanced theological study in the Middle Ages. Ignatius undertook an ambitious program, it would seem, but he didn't pursue it formally or systematically.

5. Ignatius's friendship with the Eguías at Alcalá is most interesting. The brother Miguel the printer in 1526, the year Ignatius came to Alcalá, published a Spanish translation of Erasmus's *Enchiridion militis christiani,* and it seems most probable that it was through this edition that Ignatius first made the acquaintance of the great humanist scholar. On this controversial relationship, which has its origin in Ignatius's reading of the *Enchiridion,* see John C. Olin, "Erasmus and St. Ignatius Loyola," in *Luther, Erasmus and the Reformation* (New York, 1969), pp. 114–33. Diego de Eguía and his brother Esteban in 1540 joined Ignatius in Rome and entered the new Society of Jesus.

in which he had various objects and gave him bed coverings of different colors and some candlesticks and other similar things. Wrapping them all in a sheet the pilgrim put them on his shoulders and went off to aid the poor.

As mentioned above, there was much hearsay throughout that entire region about the things happening at Alcalá; one person said one thing, and another, something else. The rumor reached the inquisitors at Toledo. When they came to Alcalá, the pilgrim was warned by their host, who told him that they were calling his companions "sack wearers" and, I believe, "enlightened ones" [*alumbrados*], and that they would make mincemeat of them.[6] So they began then to carry out their investigation and inquiry into their life; but at last they returned to Toledo without summoning them, though they had come for that reason alone. They left the trial to the vicar Figueroa, who is now with the emperor.[7] A few days later he summoned them and told them how an investigation and inquiry into their life had been made by the inquisitors and that no error had been found in their teaching nor in their life, and therefore they could do the same as they had been doing without any interference. But since they were not religious, it did not seem right for them all to go about in one habit. It would be better, and he so commanded them, if two of them, pointing to the pilgrim and Arteaga, were to dye their clothing black, and if the other two, Calixto and Cáceres, were to dye it brown; Juanico, who was a French lad, could stay as he was.

6. "Enlightened ones" or *alumbrados* were those in a religious movement known as Illuminism. Its general tendency was to seek and stress inward religious inspiration to the exclusion oftentimes of an external or formal religious practice. In the mid-1520s the authorities were beginning to crack down on its devotees, seeing or fearing an affinity with Lutheran ideas. Ignatius, a layman engaging in the apostolate he now describes, obviously came under suspicion at Alcalá, and in November 1526 the Inquisition made an investigation. It is his first brush (several more will follow) with that tribunal. See John E. Longhurst, "Saint Ignatius at Alcalá, 1526–27," *Archivum Historicum Societatis Iesu*, 26 (1957): 252–56; Longhurst, *Luther's Ghost in Spain* (Lawrence, Kansas, 1969), pp. 103–108; and Marcel Bataillon, *Erasme et l'Espagne* (Paris, 1937), pp. 65–75, 179–205.

7. Juan Rodriguez de Figueroa was then the vicar general in Alcalá of the Archbishop of Toledo, Alfonso de Fonseca. He later held high office in the service of Charles V.

The pilgrim said that they would do what they were ordered. "But," he said, "I do not know what benefit these inquisitions have; the other day a priest did not want to give the sacrament to one of us because he went to communion every eight days, and they have caused me difficulty too. We would like to know if they have found any heresy among us." "No," said Figueroa, "for if they had, they would have burned you." "They would also burn you," said the pilgrim, "if they found heresy in you." They dyed their clothing, as they had been ordered, and fifteen or twenty days later, Figueroa ordered the pilgrim not to go barefoot but to wear shoes. He did so readily, as he did in all matters of this sort when he was ordered.

Four months later Figueroa himself again began an investigation of them. Besides the usual reasons, I believe there was also the instance of a married woman of quality who had special devotion for the pilgrim. In order not to be seen, she came to the hospital in the morning at dawn, wearing a veil, as is the custom in Alcalá de Henares. On entering she removed her veil and went to the pilgrim's room. But they did nothing to them this time, nor did they summon them after the investigation had been finished, nor did they say anything to them.

Four months after that, when he was then living in a small hut outside the hospital, a policeman came to his door one day and called him, saying, "Come with me a while." He put him in jail and said to him, "You may not leave here until you are ordered to do otherwise." This was in the summertime, and, as he was not confined, many people came to visit him. He did the same things as when he was free, teaching and giving the exercises. Although many offered their services, he did not want to have an advocate or attorney. He especially remembers Doña Teresa de Cárdenas who sent someone to visit him and frequently offered to get him out, but he accepted nothing, always answering, "He for whose love I entered here will get me out, if He is served thereby."

He was in prison seventeen days without being examined or knowing the reason for it. At the end of that time Figueroa came to the jail and examined him about many things, even asking him if he observed the sabbath, and whether he knew two particular women, a mother and her daughter. To this he answered yes. [Figueroa then asked] whether he had known of their departure before they had set out. By the oath he had sworn, he said no. The vicar then placed his hand on his shoulder with a show of pleasure and said to him, "This was the reason why you were brought here." Among the many persons who followed the pilgrim there were a mother and her daughter, both widowed. The daughter was very young and very beautiful. They had entered deeply into the spirit, especially the daughter. Although they were noble women, they had gone to the Veronica of Jaén alone and on foot, though I do not know whether they were begging.[8] This caused considerable gossip in Alcalá, and Doctor Ciruelo, who had some responsibility for them, thought that the prisoner had persuaded them and for this reason had him arrested.[9] Having heard what the vicar said, the prisoner said to him, "Would you like me to speak a bit more about this affair?" He said, "yes." "Then you should know," said the prisoner, "that these two women have often emphasized to me their desire to go about the world serving the poor in one hospital and then in another. I have always dissuaded them from this idea, because the daughter is so young and beautiful and so forth, and I have told them that when they wanted to visit the poor, they could do so in Alcalá and could accompany the most holy sacrament." When this conversation was finished Figueroa left with his notary who had written it all down.

   At that time Calixto was in Segovia, and, learning of his imprisonment, he came at once, though he had recently recovered from a serious illness, and he went into the jail with him. But he [the pilgrim] told him it would be better to present himself to the vicar, who treated him kindly and told him he would order him put in jail. He would have to remain there until those women returned to see

8. The two women had gone on a fairly extended pilgrimage to the shrine of the alleged veil of St. Veronica that was venerated at Jaén in southern Spain.
9. Pedro Ciruelo, who so blamed Ignatius for the departure of his two friends (or perhaps wards), occupied the chair of Thomist theology at the University of Alcalá at this time. He was a noted scholar, philosopher, and mathematician, had formerly been at Paris, and was later to go to the University of Salmanca.

whether they would confirm what he had said. Calixto stayed in the jail a few days, but when the pilgrim saw that he was ruining his health, because he was still not entirely recovered, he had him released through the help of a doctor, a very good friend of his.

From the day the pilgrim entered jail until they let him out, forty-two days passed. At the end of that time, as the two devout women returned, the notary came to the jail to read the sentence:[10] he should go free, but they should dress like the other students and should not speak about matters of faith until they had studied for four more years, because they had no learning. For in truth, the pilgrim was the one who knew the most, though his learning had little foundation. This was the first thing he used to say whenever they examined him.

Because of this sentence he was somewhat doubtful what he should do, since it seemed they were closing the door for him to help souls, without giving him any reason except that he had not studied. At last he decided to go to Fonseca, the archbishop of Toledo, and put the case in his hands.[11] He set out from Alcalá and found the archbishop in Valladolid. Faithfully recounting the affair to him, he said that, even though he was not now in his jurisdiction nor obliged to abide by the sentence, still he would do whatever he commanded (he spoke familiarly to him, as he used to do with everyone). The archbishop received him very well and, understanding that he wanted to go to Salamanca, he said that he also had friends and a college in Salamanca and offered everything to him, and then, as he was leaving, he gave him four *escudos*.

10. The date of the sentencing and Ignatius's release was June 1, 1527. *FN*, I, 450, n.31.

11. Alfonso de Fonseca held the primatial see of Toledo from 1523 to his death in 1534. Like Ximenes before him, he was a generous patron of learning and a friend of Erasmus and the Spanish Erasmians, including the Alcalá printer, Miguel de Eguía. *Opus epistolarum Erasmi*, eds. P. S. and H. M. Allen, VI, 410. Ignatius found him at Valladolid in mid-1527 where he had gone for the baptism of the new-born son of Charles V, the future Philip II.

CHAPTER 7

Trouble at Salamanca
(July–Late 1527)

After coming to Salamanca, while he was praying in a church, a devout lady recognized him as belonging to the company [*compañía*], for his four companions had been there already for some days. She asked him his name and then took him to the lodging of his companions. When the sentence had been given in Alcalá that they should dress like students, the pilgrim said, "When you ordered us to dye our clothing, we did so; but now we cannot do this, because we do not have the wherewithal to buy clothes." So the vicar himself had provided them with clothing and caps and all the other student gear. Dressed in this fashion they had left Alcalá.

At Salamanca he confessed to a Dominican friar at San Esteban.[1] Ten or twelve days after his arrival the confessor said to him one day, "The fathers of the house would like to speak with you." He said, "In the name of God." "Then," said the confessor, "it would be good if you would come here to eat on Sunday; but I warn you of one thing, that they will want to know many things about you." So

1. San Esteban was a famous Dominican priory. Among its members were some of the University of Salamanca's greatest professors, notably at this time "the father of international law" and one of the major figures in the revival of Thomism in the sixteenth century, Francisco de Vitoria (1480–1546). Having recently returned from Paris, he occupied the "first" chair of theology at Salamanca from 1526 on.

on Sunday he went with Calixto. After eating, the subprior, in the absence of the prior, together with his confessor and I think with another friar, went with them to the chapel. With great kindness the subprior began to say what good reports they had of their life and customs: that they went about preaching in an apostolic manner and that they would be pleased to learn about these things in greater detail. So he began to ask what they had studied. The pilgrim replied, "Of all of us, I am the one who has studied the most," and he gave a clear account of the little he had studied and of the meager foundation he had.

"Well, then, what do you preach?" "We do not preach," said the pilgrim, "but we do speak familiarly with some people about the things of God; for example, after eating with some people who may invite us." "But," said the friar, "what things of God do you speak about? That is what we would like to know." "We speak," said the pilgrim, "sometimes about one virtue, sometimes about another, praising it; sometimes about one vice, sometimes about another, condemning it." "You are not educated men," said the friar, "and you speak about virtues and vices, but no one can speak about these except in one of two ways: either through education or through the Holy Spirit. If not through education, then through the Holy Spirit." Here the pilgrim was a bit beside himself because that kind of argument did not seem good to him. After being silent a while, he said it was not necessary to speak further of these matters. The friar insisted, "Well, now that there are so many errors of Erasmus and of so many others who have deceived the world, don't you wish to explain what you say?"[2]

The pilgrim said, "Father, I will say no more than I have said,

2. Erasmus was under sharp attack in Spain at this time, though he also had his staunch Spanish supporters and disciples. In the spring and summer of 1527 a conference of theologians had been held at Valladolid to examine certain charges being made against Erasmus. The Salamanca Dominicans, as well as the aforementioned Alcalá theologian Ciruelo, were prominent among his accusers. The conference was suspended in August by the Grand Inquisitor with no decision being reached, a victory in a sense for Erasmus and his friends. See Bataillon, *Erasme et l'Espagne*, chapter 5.

except before my superiors who can oblige me to do so." Before this the friar had asked why Calixto came dressed as he was; he wore a short sack and a large hat on his head, with a staff in his hand and boots almost halfway up his leg. As he was very big, he seemed more deformed. The pilgrim related how they had been imprisoned in Alcalá and had been ordered to dress like students and that his companion, because of the great heat, had given his long gown to a poor cleric. Here the friar growled between his teeth, indicating that he was not pleased, "Charity begins at home."

Now returning to the tale, the subprior, unable to get any other word out of the pilgrim but that, said, "Now remain here, for we will easily make you tell all." Then all the friars left with some haste. The pilgrim first asked if they wanted them to remain in that chapel, or where did they want them to remain. The subprior answered that they should remain in the chapel. The friars then closed all the doors and, as it appears, discussed the affair with the judges.[3] The two of them were in the monastery for three days, eating in the refectory with the friars, though nothing was said to them in the name of the court. Their room was almost always full of friars who came to see them. The pilgrim always spoke as was his custom; as a result there was already some division among them, many showing that they were sympathetic to them.

At the end of three days a notary came and took them to jail. They did not put them down below with the criminals but in an upper room, where, because it was old and unused, there was a lot of dirt. They were both bound with the same chain, each one by his foot. The chain was hooked to a post in the middle of the house and was ten or thirteen palms long. Each time that one wanted to do something, the other had to accompany him. All that night they kept a vigil. The next day when their imprisonment was known in the city, people sent them something on which to sleep in jail and every necessity in abundance. Many people came con-

---

3. These were evidently judges in the ecclesiastical court at Salamanca, and the discussion must have been on the question of proceeding against Ignatius and Calixto.

tinually to visit them, and the pilgrim continued his exercises, speaking about God and the like.

The bachelor Frías came to examine each of them separately, and the pilgrim gave him all his papers containing the exercises so they could examine them.[4] Asked if they had companions, they said they did and told where they were. On the bachelor's orders they went there and brought Cáceres and Arteaga to jail, but they left Juanico, who later became a friar. But they did not put them above with the other two but down below where the common prisoners were. Here, too, he did not want to have an advocate or attorney.

Some days later he was summoned before four judges, the three doctors, Sanctisidoro, Paravinhas, and Frías, and the fourth was the bachelor Frías. All of them had now seen the exercises. Here they asked him many things not only about the exercises, but also about theology; for example, about the Trinity and the Eucharist and how he understood those articles. First he made his preface and then, commanded by the judges, he spoke in such a manner that they had no reason to condemn him. The bachelor Frías who had always intervened in these matters more than the others, also asked him about a case in canon law. He was required to answer everything, but he always said first that he did not know what scholars said about those matters. Then they commanded him to explain the first commandment the way he usually explained it. He started to do so and said so many things about the first commandment that they had no desire to ask him more. Before this, when they were speaking about the exercises, they insisted a good deal on one point only, which was at the beginning: when a thought is a venial sin and when it is mortal.[5] The reason was that he, though uneducated, was deciding it. He answered, "If this is true or not, resolve it now; and if it is not

4. Frías was vicar general of the bishop of Salamanca and also a professor of theology at the university. The "papers containing the exercises" refer, of course, to Ignatius's spiritual exercises or to a very early version of the same. It is the first indication of their having been written.

5. Cf. *Spiritual Exercises*, pp. 18–9.

true, condemn it." But in the end they left without condemning anything.

Among the many who came to speak to him in jail, Don Francisco de Mendoza, who is now Cardinal of Burgos, came one time with the bachelor Frías. In a kindly manner he asked him how he was getting on in prison and if it bothered him to be a prisoner. He replied, "I will answer what I answered today to a lady who, on seeing me in prison, spoke words of compassion." I said to her, "By this you show that you do not wish to be imprisoned for the love of God. Does imprisonment seem to be such a great evil to you? Well, I will tell you that there are not so many grills and chains in Salamanca that I would not wish for more for the love of God."

At this time it happened that all the prisoners in the jail fled, but the two companions who were with them did not flee. In the morning when they were found there alone without anyone, with the doors open, everyone was deeply edified, and there was much talk in the city; so they gave them an entire palace that was near there as a prison.

After twenty-two days of imprisonment, they were summoned to hear the sentence, which was that no error was found in their life or teaching. Therefore they could do what they had been doing, teaching doctrine and speaking about the things of God, so long as they never defined that "this is a mortal sin or this is a venial sin," until they had studied for four more years. After the sentence was read, the judges displayed great kindness, because they wanted it to be accepted. The pilgrim said that he would do everything the sentence ordered, but that he would not accept it, because, without condemning him for anything, they closed his mouth so that he could not help his neighbors insofar as he was able. Although Doctor Frías urged him and showed that he was very benevolent, the pilgrim said no more except that, as long as he was in the jurisdiction of Salamanca, he would do what had been ordered. Then they were released from jail, and he began to commend himself to God and to think about what he ought to do. He found great difficulty in remaining in Salamanca, for in the matter of helping souls it seemed to him that the door had been closed by this prohibition not to define mortal and venial sin.

So he decided to go to Paris to study. When the pilgrim was considering at Barcelona whether he should study and how much, his entire concern was whether, after he had studied, he should enter religion or go about the world. When thoughts of entering religion came to him, then he also had the desire to enter a corrupted and poorly reformed order so that he would suffer more in it. He also thought that perhaps God would help them. God gave him great confidence that he would endure easily all the insults and injuries they did to him.

Now at the time of his imprisonment in Salamanca the same desire that he had to help souls, and for that reason to study first and to gather some others for the same purpose and to keep those he had, did not fail him. Resolving to go to Paris, he arranged with them [his companions] to wait there while he went to see if he could find some means by which they could study.

Many important persons strongly insisted that he should not go, but they could never dissuade him. Fifteen or twenty days after leaving prison, he set out alone, taking some books, on a little donkey. When he arrived at Barcelona all those who knew him advised him against the journey to France because of the great wars there, recounting many specific examples, even telling him that they put Spaniards on roasting spits, but he never had any kind of fear.

In æde suburbana B Virginis ipse, ac focij certo fe voto obftringunt diuinam vbique gloriam, animarūq̃ salutem in Hierofolymitana præfertim expeditione pro-curandi, ac palmam inde martyrij sedulo conqui-rendi, quod votum ibidem quotannis renouant.

4)

Ignatius and companions at the Mass of Peter Faber following their vows in Paris, August 15, 1534.

CHAPTER 8

At the University of Paris
(February 1528–March 1535)

So he set out for Paris, alone and on foot. He reached Paris in the month of February more or less, and, as he told me, it was in the year 1528 or 1527.[1] He lodged in a house with some Spaniards and went to study humanities at Montaigu.[2] The reason was that they had made him advance with so much haste in his studies that he was found to be very deficient in fundamentals. He studied with young boys, following the order and method of Paris. When he first came to Paris a merchant gave him twenty-five *èscudos* for a bill of exchange from Barcelona, which sum he gave to one of the Spaniards in the lodging house to keep; but in a short time the latter spent them and had nothing to pay him with. So after Lent the pilgrim had

1. Ignatius arrived in Paris on February 2, 1528, as we learn from a letter he wrote to his friend and benefactress back in Barcelona, Inés Pascual. Rahner, *Saint Ignatius Loyola, Letters to Women*, pp. 180–81.
2. The college of Montaigu was one of the more than fifty colleges that comprised the University of Paris at this time. It had been restored and reestablished by its famous principal John Standonck in the late fifteenth century, and it had a reputation for austerity and discipline. Erasmus attended it to his dismay in the 1490s, and John Calvin had just completed his studies there for the master of arts prior to Ignatius's arrival. L. Rodriguez-Grahit, "Ignace de Loyola et le college Montaigu. L'influence de Standonck sur Ignace," *Bibliothèque d'humanisme et renaissance* 20 (1958): 388–401; and Robert Rouquette, S.J., "Ignace de Loyola dans le Paris intellectual du XVIe siècle," *Études* 290 (1956): 18–40.

nothing left because he had spent the money and because of the reason mentioned above. He was compelled to beg and also to leave the house where he was living.

He was received in the hospice of St. Jacques, beyond the [church of the] Innocents. It was very inconvenient for study because the hospice was a good distance from the college of Montaigu, and it was necessary to return at the sound of the Ave Maria in order to find the door open and to leave at daybreak. Thus he could not attend very well at his lessons.[3] Having to seek alms to support himself was another difficulty. Almost five years had passed now since he had had stomach pains, so he began to subject himself to greater penances and abstinences. Spending some time in this life at the hospice and begging and seeing that he was making little progress in his studies, he began to wonder what he should do. Seeing that there were some who served some of the regents in the colleges and had time to study, he decided to seek a master.

He kept this consideration and intention to himself and found great consolation in it, imagining that the master would be Christ, that one of the students would be called St. Peter and another St. John, and so with each one of the apostles. "When the master commands me, I will think that Christ commands me; when someone else commands me, I will think that St. Peter commands me." He worked very hard to find a master; on the one hand he spoke to the bachelor Castro and also to a Carthusian friar who knew many professors and to others, but it was not possible for him to find a master.

At last, having found no solution, a Spanish friar told him one day that it would be better for him to go each year to Flanders and spend two months or even less, in order to obtain the wherewithal so he could study the whole year. After commending this idea to God, it seemed good to him. Following this advice, each year he brought

3. The hours at the hospice were such that he couldn't attend all his classes at Montaigu. He had to be in before dark and couldn't leave before daybreak. The first class at Montaigu was at 5:00 A.M., and the scholastic day ended with a repetition or review at 7:00 P.M.

back from Flanders the means to sustain himself in some way.[4] Once he went over to England and got more alms than he used to get in other years.

The first time he returned from Flanders he began to give himself more intensively than ever to spiritual conversations, and he gave the exercises simultaneously to three persons, namely, Peralta, the bachelor Castro who was at the Sorbonne, and a Vizcayan who was at Sainte-Barbe named Amador.[5] They changed very much and gave all they had to the poor, even their books, and began to seek alms throughout Paris. They went to live in the hospice of St. Jacques, where the pilgrim had stayed before but had now left for the reasons mentioned above. This caused great excitement in the university, for the first two were notable persons and were very well known. The Spaniards then began to argue with the two masters but, not being able to convince them by many reasons and arguments to return to the university, many of them came one day with armed force and dragged them out of the hospice.

Brought to the university, they agreed that they would carry out their plans after they had finished their studies. The bachelor Castro later returned to Spain and preached at Burgos for some time and then became a Carthusian friar at Valencia. Peralta set out on foot as a pilgrim to Jerusalem. In this way he was captured in Italy by a captain, a relative of his, who took steps to bring him to the pope who ordered him to return to Spain. These events did not happen immediately but some years later. Great murmurings arose in Paris, especially among the Spaniards, against the pilgrim. Our Master de

4. Ignatius's begging tours took him to Antwerp and Bruges, where there were many Spanish merchants. On one of his trips, possibly in the summer of 1529, he met and dined at the home of the famous Spanish humanist Juan Luis Vives in Bruges. On this meeting see Olin, "Erasmus and St. Ignatius Loyola," in *Luther, Erasmus and the Reformation,* pp. 123–24.

5. Sainte-Barbe is the college of Sainte-Barbe, a neighbor and rival of the college of Montaigu in Paris. Ignatius himself will transfer there from Montaigu in the fall of 1529. Its principal in these years was the Portuguese doctor of theology Diego de Gouvea whom Ignatius will refer to in the next paragraph. There were many Spanish and Portuguese students at Sainte-Barbe, the king of Portugal having established fifty scholarships there just a few years before.

Gouvea said that he had caused Amador, who was in his college, to go mad; he decided, and he said so, that the first time he [Ignatius] came to Sainte-Barbe he would give him a beating as a seducer of the students.

The Spaniard with whom he had stayed at the beginning and who had spent his money without paying it back, set out for Spain by way of Rouen. While awaiting passage at Rouen he fell ill. The pilgrim learned from his letter that he was ill and felt the desire to go to see him and help him. He also thought that at that meeting he could persuade him to leave the world and give himself up completely to the service of God.

In order to obtain this he felt the desire to walk the twenty-eight leagues from Paris to Rouen in his bare feet without eating or drinking. As he prayed for this he found that he was very much afraid. At last he went to [the church of] St. Dominic, where he decided to walk in the manner mentioned above. The great fear he had of tempting God had now passed.

He got up early the next day, the morning that he was going to set out. As he began to dress, such a great fear came over him that he seemed almost unable to dress himself. Before it was dawn he left the house and the city too, still with that repugnance. The fear always remained with him and persisted as far as Argenteuil, a walled town three leagues from Paris on the way to Rouen, where the garments of Our Lord are said to be kept. He passed the town with some spiritual travail, but as he climbed up a hill that fear began to go away. He felt great consolation and spiritual strength with such joy that he began to shout through the fields and to speak with God and so forth. He lodged that night with a poor beggar in a hospital, having traveled fourteen leagues that day. The next day he walked until he found refuge in a straw hut. The third day he reached Rouen. All this time he went without eating or drinking and barefoot, as he had planned. In Rouen he consoled the sick man and helped him board a ship going to Spain. He also gave him letters addressed to the companions who were in Salamanca, namely, Calixto, Cáceres, and Arteaga.

Not to have to speak further of these companions, their lot was this: While the pilgrim was in Paris he wrote frequently to them, as they had agreed, about the difficulty they would have in coming to Paris to study. But he also undertook to write to Doña Leonor de Mascarenhas to assist Calixto with letters to the court of the king of Portugal, so he could obtain one of the scholarships which the king of Portugal gave in Paris.[6] Doña Leonor gave Calixto the letters and a mule to ride and *quatrini* for his expenses. Calixto went to the court of the king of Portugal, but in the end he did not come to Paris; rather, returning to Spain he went to the India of the Emperor[7] with a certain spiritual lady. He returned to Spain later but went to the same India again and then returned to Spain a rich man. He caused astonishment in Salamanca to all those who had known him before.

Cáceres returned to Segovia, his native place, and there began to live in such a manner that he seemed to have forgotten his initial intention.

Arteaga was made a *comendador*. Later when the Society was already in Rome, he was given a bishopric in India. He wrote to the pilgrim to give it to one of the Society, but the answer was in the negative, so he went to the India of the Emperor as a bishop and died there in strange circumstances, that is, when he was ill there were two water glasses to refresh him, one with water which the doctor had ordered for him, the other with water of *solimano,* a poison. The latter was given him by mistake and killed him.

The pilgrim returned to Paris from Rouen and discovered that because of the previous affair of Castro and Peralta a great rumor had started about him and that the inquisitor had inquired about him. But he did not want to wait longer and went to the inquisitor, telling him that he understood he was looking for him and that he

6. Doña Leonor de Mascarenhas (1503–84) was of the high Portuguese nobility and at this time a lady-in-waiting of Queen Isabella of Spain, the Portuguese Infanta who had married the Emperor Charles V in 1526. She was the governess of the young Philip II and a lifelong friend of Ignatius and the Society of Jesus. Ignatius apparently met her in 1526–27, possibly at Valladolid when he went there to see Archbishop Fonseca. See Rahner, *Saint Ignatius Loyola, Letters to Women,* pp. 417ff.

7. To Spanish America, probably Mexico.

was prepared for anything he might wish. The inquisitor was our Master Ory, a Dominican friar.[8] He [Ignatius] begged him to expedite it at once because he wanted to enter the arts course on St. Remy's Day. He wanted to get this business over first so he would be better able to attend to his studies. The inquisitor did not summon him again but told him it was true that they had spoken of his doings and so on.

A short time after this came the feast of St. Remy at the beginning of October, and he entered the arts course under a teacher named Master Juan Peña.[9] He entered with the intention of keeping those who had decided to follow the Lord, but he would not go about anymore in search of others, so that he could study more easily.

As he began to listen to the lectures of the course, the same temptations that had beset him when he studied grammar in Barcelona began to come to him. Every time he heard the lectures, he could not pay attention because of the many spiritual thoughts that occurred to him. Realizing that in this way he made little progress in study, he went to his master and promised him never to fail to hear the whole course, so long as he could find bread and water to support himself. After making this promise all those devotions which came to him at the wrong time left him, and he went on peacefully with his studies. At this time he became acquainted with Master Peter Faber and Master Francis Xavier, whom he later won for God's service by means of the exercises.[10]

8. Matthieu Ory was then prior of the Dominican convent on the rue Saint-Jacques. He had been appointed inquisitor in Paris by Pope Clement VII in 1528 in the effort to check the spread of the new Lutheran doctrines. His title "our Master," *magister noster,* (like that of Diego de Gouvea several paragraphs above), was the usual one for a Paris theologian.

9. Ignatius shifted on October 1, 1529, from Montaigu to the college of Sainte-Barbe, and it is from the latter school that he received his master of arts in 1534. The shift is most interesting, for Sainte-Barbe was a more liberal college than Montaigu and a crossroads in Paris at this time for the two prevalent intellectual currents—the scholastic and the humanist. See H. Bernard-Maitre, S.J., "Les fondateurs de la Compagnie de Jésus et l'humanisme parisien de la Renaissance," *Nouvelle revue théologique,* 72 (1950): 811–33, and Marcel Bataillon, *Etudes sur le Portugal au temps de l'humanisme* (Coimbra, 1952), pp. 109–29.

10. Peter Faber or Pierre Favre (1506–46) and Francis Xavier (1506–52) became

At that stage in his course they did not persecute him as before. On this point Doctor Frago once said to him that he marveled that he went about peacefully, without anyone giving him trouble, and he replied, "The reason is because I do not speak to anyone of the things of God, but when I have finished the course I will return to my custom."[11]

While the two were speaking together a friar came to ask Doctor Frago to try to find him a house, because in the one where he had his lodging many people had died of the plague, it was thought, for the plague was then spreading in Paris. Doctor Frago and the pilgrim wished to go to see the house. They took a woman who understood these matters very well, and on entering within she affirmed that it was the plague. The pilgrim also wanted to enter. Finding a sick person, he comforted him and touched his sore with his hand. After he had comforted and encouraged him a while, he went out alone. His hand began to hurt so that it seemed he had caught the plague. This thought was so strong that he could not overcome it until he thrust his hand forcefully into his mouth and moved it about inside, saying, "If I have the plague in my hand, I will also have it in my mouth." When he had done this, the thought left him and the pain left his hand.

But when he returned to the college of Sainte-Barbe where he then had lodging and was attending the course, those in the college who knew that he had entered the house of the plague fled before him and did not want to let him enter. So he was forced to remain outside for a few days.

It is the custom at Paris for those who are studying arts in the third

---

two of Ignatius's most important disciples and were founder members with him of the Society of Jesus. Faber came from a mountain village in Haute Savoie, Xavier, from a castle in Navarre. Both entered Sainte-Barbe in 1525 and were nearing the completion of their arts course when Ignatius came on the scene in 1529. We learn from Faber's autobiographical *Memorial* (*FN*, I, 32) that he and Xavier shared a room at Sainte-Barbe and that Ignatius joined them when he entered the college on October 1, 1529. Faber also tutored Ignatius in his studies at the behest of their common master Peña. For further introduction to Faber and Xavier, see James Brodrick, S.J., *The Origin of the Jesuits* (New York, 1940).

11. Doctor Frago has been identified as a professor of Scripture at the Sorbonne.

year, in order to receive the baccalaureate, "to take a stone," as they say.[12] Some very poor students, however, could not do it because they had to spend an *escudo* for it. The pilgrim began to wonder whether it would be wise for him to do so. Finding himself in great doubt and irresolute, he decided to put the matter in the hands of his master, who advised him to take it, and he did so. There were not lacking, however, some critics; at least one Spaniard commented upon it.

Now at this time in Paris he was very sick in his stomach, and every fifteen days he had a stomachache which lasted a good hour and gave him a fever. Once the stomachache lasted sixteen or seventeen hours. At this time he had already finished the arts course and had studied theology for a few years and had gathered the companions.[13] His illness continued to get worse, but he could not find a cure, though many were tried.

The doctors said that nothing else but his native air could help him. The companions gave him the same advice and did so with great insistence. Now at this time they had all decided what they had to do, namely, to go to Venice and then to Jerusalem to spend their lives in the service of souls; and if they were not given permission to remain in Jerusalem, they would return to Rome and present

12. The meaning of the expression "to take a stone" is not clear. It may refer to the baccalaureate exam.

13. Ignatius finished the arts course at Sainte-Barbe in late 1532, was examined for the licentiate in 1533, and received his masters degree in 1534. He had meanwhile begun to study theology at the Dominican convent on the rue Saint-Jacques, a famous school where a revival of Thomism had been inaugurated in the earlier years of the century by Pierre Crockaert and his more renowned pupil Francisco de Vitoria. See Dudon, *St. Ignatius of Loyola*, pp. 135–45; Rouquette, "Ignace de Loyola dans le Paris intellectuel," and M.-D. Chenu, O.P., "L'humanisme et la Réforme au collège de Saint-Jacques de Paris," *Archives d'histoire dominicaine* I (1946): 130–54.

Ignatius had gathered six companions by late 1534—all students like himself in Paris, though all a good deal younger than himself. They were, besides Faber and Xavier, Diego Lainez, Alfonso Salmeron, and Nicholas Bobadilla, three Spaniards, and Simon Rodrigues, a Portuguese who had come on a royal scholarship to Sainte-Barbe. On August 15, 1534, Ignatius and his six friends took a vow in a chapel on Montmartre to go to Jerusalem—an event that has sometimes been viewed as the beginning of the Society of Jesus. *FN*, I, 36–39. Ignatius explains this decision in the next paragraph.

themselves to the vicar of Christ, so that he could make use of them wherever he thought it would be to the greater glory of God and the service of souls. They also planned to wait a year in Venice for passage, but if there was no passage for the East that year, they would be free of their vow to go to Jerusalem and would go to the pope and so on.

At last the pilgrim let himself be persuaded by the companions and also because the Spaniards among them had various matters to attend to which he could settle. It was agreed that when he felt well he should go and settle their affairs and then proceed to Venice where he would wait for the companions.

This was the year 1535, and the companions were to set out, according to the agreement, in the year 1537 on the feast of the conversion of St. Paul;[14] but because of the war that broke out, they left in November in the year 1536. As the pilgrim was about to set out, he learned that he had been accused before the inquisitor and that an action had been started against him. Knowing this but seeing that they did not summon him, he went to the inquisitor and told him what he had heard and that he was about to set out for Spain and that he had companions. He asked him to pass sentence. The inquisitor said it was true that an accusation had been made but that it did not seem to him to be anything of importance. He only wanted to see his book of exercises. When he saw them he praised them very much and asked the pilgrim to let him have a copy of them. This he did. Nevertheless he again insisted that the case be continued until sentence was passed; but the inquisitor did not want to do so, so he [Ignatius] brought a notary public and witnesses to his house and took down a record of this whole affair.

14. January 25.

CHAPTER 9

Revisiting Spain
(April–Late 1535)

With that done, he mounted a small horse the companions had bought and set out alone for his homeland.[1] Along the way he felt much better. When he arrived in his province, he left the main road and took the mountain road, which was more lonely. As he journeyed along a short while, he met two armed men who together advanced toward him (that road is somewhat notorious for assassins). After he had passed them by a bit, they turned about and followed him with great haste, and he was somewhat afraid. But he spoke to them and learned that they were servants of his brother, who had sent them to find him, because, as it seems, he had had news of his coming from Bayonne in France, where the pilgrim was recognized. So they went along, and he went along the same road. He met them traveling together a short ways before he arrived in that region. They were very insistent that he go to his brother's house, but they could not force him. Thus, he went to the hospital and later at a convenient time went to seek alms in the area.[2]

---

1. Ignatius left Paris the end of March 1535 for his native Guipúzcoa in northern Spain. After crossing the frontier near Irun he headed for and stayed in the town of Azpeitia. The distance from Paris is about 550 miles, and it took Ignatius a good month to make the journey.
2. The brother Ignatius refers to is an elder brother, Martín García, then resident

In this hospital he began to speak of the things of God with many people who came to visit him, and by His grace he gathered much fruit. As soon as he arrived he decided to teach Christian doctrine every day to children but his brother roundly objected to this, saying that no one would come. He replied that one would be enough. But after he began to do it, many came continually to hear him, and even his brother did so.[3]

Besides Christian doctrine, he also preached on Sundays and feast days for the service and help of the souls of those who came many miles to hear him. He also made an attempt to eliminate some abuses, and with God's help he put order into some. For example, he caused gambling to be strictly forbidden; he persuaded the man responsible for justice to do that. There was also another abuse there. The young girls in that region always went about with their heads uncovered and did not cover them until they were married. But there were many women who had become concubines of priests and other men and who were as faithful to them as though they were their wives. This was so common that the concubines were not at all ashamed to say that they had covered their heads for so and so, and they were known as belonging to so and so.

Much evil arose from this custom. The pilgrim persuaded the governor to make a law that all those who covered their heads for anyone and who were not their wives should be legally punished. In this way this abuse began to be overcome. He caused the order

---

in the family castle at Loyola. Ignatius chose to stay not at his former home but at the hospital of the Magdalena, actually a kind of poorhouse, in nearby Azpeitia.

3. This first activity of Ignatius at Azpeitia became one of the primary purposes of the Society of Jesus when it was organized in 1539–40. Ignatius's concern for instructing the young in Christian doctrine (as well as the objection of his brother) recalls a discussion on this topic that Erasmus relates in a letter to Colet. Erasmus, defending such instruction, argued "that Christ did not despise the very young, and that no age of man was more deserving of generous help, and nowhere could a richer harvest be anticipated, since the young are the growing crop and growing timber of the commonwealth; I added all who are truly religious hold the view that no service is more likely to gain merit in God's eyes than the leading of children to Christ." H. C. Porter, ed., *Erasmus and Cambridge: the Cambridge Letters of Erasmus*, trans. D. F. S. Thomson (Toronto, 1963), p. 122.

to be given that the poor should be provided for publicly and regularly[4] and that bells should be rung three times for the *Ave Maria,* that is, in the morning, at noon, and in the evening so that the people might pray as in Rome. Although he felt well at the beginning, he later fell gravely ill. After he was cured, he decided to set out to take care of those affairs his companions had entrusted to him and to set out without *quatrini.* For this reason his brother was very upset and was ashamed that he wanted to go on foot. In the evening the pilgrim was willing to agree to journey on horseback with his brother and his relatives to the border of the province.

But when he left the province he jumped to his feet without taking anything and went to Pamplona and thence to Almazán, Father Lainez's hometown, and then to Sigüenza and Toledo and from Toledo to Valencia.[5] In all these native places of his companions he did not want to take anything, although with great insistence they offered him very much.

In Valencia he spoke with Castro who was a Carthusian monk. He wanted to sail to Genoa but the devout people of Valencia begged him not to do so because they said that Barbarossa was on the sea with many ships and so on. Although they said many things, enough to make him afraid, nevertheless nothing could make him hesitate.

Setting sail in a large ship, he passed through the storm mentioned above, where he said that he was on the verge of death three times.[6] When he arrived at Genoa he took the road to Bologna, on which he suffered very much, especially one time when he lost his way and began to journey along a riverbank down below. The road was up above, but as he went farther along the path began to get narrower; and it became so narrow that he could no longer go forward nor turn back. He began to crawl along and in this way he covered a good

4. Ignatius's efforts here are quite notable. The town council of Azpeitia passed several ordinances prohibiting begging and providing regular assistance for those in need. Dudon, *St. Ignatius of Loyola,* pp. 165–66.

5. Ignatius visited Xavier's brother in Navarre, Laínez's parents at Almazán, and Salmeron's family at Toledo. He left Valencia in the fall of 1535 for Italy.

6. See p. 40.

distance with great fear, because each time he moved he thought he would fall into the river. This was the greatest toil and bodily travail that he had ever had, but at last he got out of it. He wanted to enter Bologna, and as he was crossing over a small wooden bridge, he fell under the bridge. Then, as he arose covered with mud and water, he made many people who were there laugh. Entering Bologna he began to seek alms, but he did not find a single *quatrino,* though he looked everywhere. He was ill for some time in Bologna, but afterwards he went to Venice in the same way as always.

CHAPTER 10

Venice and Vicenza
(Late 1535–Late 1537)

During that time in Venice he busied himself giving the exercises and in other spiritual conversations. The most distinguished persons to whom he gave them were Master Pietro Contarini and Master Gasparo de Doctis and a Spaniard whose name was Roças. There was also another Spaniard there called the bachelor Hoces, who talked a good deal with the pilgrim and also with the bishop of Ceuta [or Chieti?]. Although he had some desire to make the exercises, nonetheless he did not put it into execution. At last he decided to make them. Three or four days after he had done so, he revealed his soul to the pilgrim, telling him that, because of the things someone had told him, he had been afraid that he would be taught some wicked doctrine in the exercises. For this reason he had carried with him certain books so he could have recourse to them, if perchance he tried to deceive him. He was helped very much by the exercises and at last he decided to follow the pilgrim's life. He was also the first one to die.[1]

In Venice the pilgrim also endured another persecution. There were many who said that his effigy had been burned in Spain and

1. Hoces died in Padua in 1538, the first to do so of the group of companions who would form the Society of Jesus.

in Paris. This affair reached such a point that a trial was held and sentence was given in favor of the pilgrim.

The nine companions came to Venice at the beginning of 1537.[2] There they separated to serve in different hospitals. After two or three months they all went to Rome to receive the blessing for the journey to Jerusalem. The pilgrim did not go because of Doctor Ortiz and also because of the new Theatine cardinal.[3] The companions returned from Rome with notes for 200 or 300 *escudos*, which had been given to them as alms for the journey to Jerusalem. They did not want to take anything but notes; later, not being able to go to Jerusalem, they returned them to those who had given them.

The companions returned to Venice in the same way they had gone, that is, on foot and begging but divided into three groups and in such a way that they were always of different nations. In Venice those who were not ordained were there ordained for mass, and the nuncio who was then in Venice (and who was later called Cardinal Verallo) gave them faculties.[4] They were ordained under the title of poverty [*ad titulum paupertatis*] and made vows of chastity and poverty.

In that year no ships sailed for the East because the Venetians had

2. In addition to the six companions of Ignatius who made their vows with him at Montmartre in 1534, three others joined the band in Paris a few years later—Claude Le Jay, Paschase Broet, and Jean Codure.

3. Dr. Pedro Ortiz was a Spanish theologian who was on an embassy in Rome for Charles V at this time. Ignatius had previously known him at the University of Paris, where the doctor apparently was one of those Spaniards who was angry at the pilgrim for the influence he had on Peralta, Castro, and Amador. The Theatine cardinal was Gian Pietro Carafa, Bishop of Chieti (or in Latin, Theate, whence the term Theatine) and one of the founders of the so-called Theatine order. He was an ardent reformer and had recently been called to Rome from Venice to serve on a papal reform commission. Pope Paul III made him a cardinal in December 1536. Ignatius had known him in Venice and evidently had some sharp disagreement with him over the character of the Theatine order. See Dudon, *St. Ignatius of Loyola*, pp. 233–35. Carafa was elected Pope Paul IV in May 1555, just a few months before Ignatius was dictating this portion of his autobiography.

4. Ignatius, Xavier, Lainez, Salmeron, Bobadilla, Rodrigues, and Codure were ordained as priests on June 24, 1537, by the bishop of Arbe. Faber, Le Jay, and Broet were already priests. The faculties given them by the nuncio authorized them to preach and explain Holy Scripture in the area of the Venetian republic.

broken with the Turks. So, seeing that their hope of sailing was far off, they dispersed throughout the Venetian territory, with the intention of waiting the year they had agreed upon; after it was finished, if there was no passage, they would go to Rome.

It fell to the pilgrim to go with Faber and Lainez to Vicenza. There they found a certain house outside the city, which had neither doors nor windows. They stayed in it, sleeping on a little bit of straw that they had brought. Two of them always went out to seek alms in the city twice a day, but they got so little they could hardly sustain themselves. They usually ate a little toasted bread when they had it, and the one who remained at home took care to toast it. In this way they spent forty days, not attending to anything other than prayer.

After the forty days Master Jean Codure arrived, and all four decided to begin to preach. All four went to different piazzas and began to preach on the same day and at the same hour, first shouting loudly and summoning the people with their hats. Their preaching caused much talk in the city, and many persons were moved with devotion, and they received in great abundance the necessities for their bodily welfare.

During the time he was at Vicenza he had many spiritual visions and ordinary consolations (quite the contrary of what he had experienced in Paris). Especially when he began to prepare for the priesthood at Venice and when he was preparing to say mass and in all his journeys he had great supernatural visitations like those he used to have when he was at Manresa. While he was still at Vicenza he learned that one of the companions, who was at Bassano, was deathly ill;[5] at the same time he was also ill with a fever. Nevertheless, he set out on the road and traveled so fast that Faber, his companion, could not keep up with him. On that journey he had assurance from God, and he told Faber so, that the companion would not die of that illness. Arriving at Bassano he comforted the sick man very much, and he quickly recovered. Then they all returned to Vicenza. All ten were there for some time, and some of them went about seeking alms in the towns near Vicenza.

5. It was Simon Rodrigues.

At last, at the end of the year, as they had not found passage, they decided to go to Rome, even the pilgrim, because on the other occasion when the companions had gone, those two about whom he had doubts had shown themselves to be very kind. Divided into three or four groups, the pilgrim with Faber and Lainez, they went to Rome. On this journey he was visited very specially by God.

After he became a priest he had decided to spend a year without saying mass, preparing himself and begging Our Lady to deign to place him with her Son. One day, while still a few miles from Rome, he was praying in a church and experienced such a change in his soul and saw so clearly that God the Father had placed him with His Son Christ that his mind could not doubt that God the Father had indeed placed him with His Son.[6]

(I, who am writing these things, said to the pilgrim, when he told me this, that Lainez had recounted it with other details as he had heard it. He told me that everything that Lainez said was true because he did not recall it in such detail, but that at the moment when he narrated it he was certain that he had said nothing but the truth. He said the same to me about other things.)

After arriving at Rome he told the companions that he saw that the windows were closed, meaning that they would have to meet many contradictions. He also said, "It is necessary that we be very careful of ourselves and that we not enter into conversations with women, unless they are prominent." Speaking about this matter, Master Francis later heard the confession of a lady in Rome and visited her a few times to discuss her spiritual affairs, and she was later found to be pregnant; but the Lord willed that the one who had done that wicked deed should be discovered. The same thing befell Jean Codure with a spiritual daughter who was found with a man.

6. This is an incident in Ignatius's life known as the vision of La Storta, and from the start Jesuit tradition has placed great importance on it. It is seen as the climax of Ignatius's ardent desire to serve God under the banner of Christ, "the mystical granting of that prayer," in the words of Father de Guibert. The promise of divine favor and protection for Ignatius and his band as they now neared the gates of Rome has also traditionally been ascribed to it. De Guibert, *The Jesuits*, pp. 37–39.

Paulus III Pont.Max. Societatis Iesu insti=
tutum ab Ignatio oblatum postquam legisset,
DIGITVS, inquit DEI EST HIC. Socie =
tatemque confirmat anno salutis 1540.

Pope Paul III confirms the Society of Jesus, 1540.

CHAPTER II

Rome
(1538)

From Rome the pilgrim went to Monte Cassino to give the exercises to Doctor Ortiz. He was there forty days during which he once saw the bachelor Hoces entering heaven. This caused him many tears and great spiritual consolation. He saw this so clearly that if he said the contrary he would appear to be lying. From Monte Cassino he brought back Francesco de Strada and returned to Rome where he busied himself helping souls. They were still living at the vineyard. He gave the spiritual exercises to different people at the same time, one of whom lived near Santa Maria Maggiore, the other at Ponte Sesto.[1]

Then the persecutions began.[2] Miguel began to give offense and

1. Cardinal Gasparo Contarini, the eminent Venetian scholar and diplomat who had been called to Rome by Paul III in 1535 to assist in the work of church reform, was one of those to whom Ignatius gave the spiritual exercises in these early months. He was related distantly to Pietro Contarini to whom Ignatius refers at the beginning of Chapter 10, and the latter had recommended Ignatius and his friends to the Cardinal after they had come to Rome. He was one of the chief supporters of the nascent Society of Jesus.

2. These "persecutions" which Ignatius and his companions suffered when they first came to Rome are described in fuller detail in a lengthy letter Ignatius sent to his friend and benefactress Isabel Roser back in Barcelona in December 1538. This interesting document which expands and supplements this section of the autobiography follows as an appendix in this volume.

to speak badly of the pilgrim, who caused him to be summoned before the governor. He first showed the governor one of Miguel's letters, in which he praised the pilgrim very much. The governor examined Miguel, and the result was to banish him from Rome.

Mudarra and Barreda then began their persecutions, saying that the pilgrim and his companions were fugitives from Spain, from Paris, and from Venice. In the end the two of them confessed in the presence of the governor and the legate, who was then in Rome, that they had nothing bad to say about them nor about their customs nor their teaching. The legate ordered silence to be imposed on the whole affair, but the pilgrim did not accept that, saying he wanted a definite sentence. This did not please the legate nor the governor nor even those who at first favored the pilgrim; but at last, after some months, the pope came to Rome.[3] The pilgrim went to speak to him at Frascati and gave him several reasons; thus informed, the pope ordered sentence to be given, and it was in his favor, and so forth.

With the help of the pilgrim and his companions some works of piety, such as the Catechumens, Santa Martha, the orphanage, and the like were begun in Rome.[4] Master Nadal can recount the rest.

On October 20, after these things had been recounted, I asked the pilgrim about the exercises and the constitutions, as I wanted to know how he had drawn them up.[5] He told me that he had not made up the exercises all at once, but that when he found some things were helpful to his soul, he thought they might also be helpful to others, and so he put them in writing, for example, the examination of

3. Paul III had been at Nice earlier in 1538 presiding at peace negotiations between Charles V and Francis I. Ignatius saw him in August at his residence at Frascati, an event he describes in his letter to Isabel Roser. Ignatius and his companions subsequently had the pope's public support.

4. Ignatius refers to some of the activities he and his companions undertook when they first came to Rome—opening a center for the religious instruction of Jewish converts, founding a house of refuge for former prostitutes, establishing an orphanage, and the like. See Dudon, *St. Ignatius of Loyola*, pp. 381ff.

5. The exercises of course are Ignatius's *Spiritual Exercises* which had been in the making since his days at Manresa in 1522. They attained their final form probably about the time he and his companions came to Rome. The earliest manuscript extant of the complete exercises dates from 1541. The constitutions are the *Constitutions of the Society of Jesus* which Ignatius began work on in 1541 but did not complete a text of until 1550. They were in their last phase of discussion and revision at this time.

conscience with that form of the lines, and so on. He told me that he derived the elections especially from that variety of spirit and thoughts which he had felt at Loyola when he was still suffering with his leg.[6] He told me he would speak to me about the constitutions in the evening.

The same day, with the air of a person who was more recollected than usual, he summoned me before supper and made a sort of protestation to me, the substance of which was to show the simplicity of intention with which he had related these things. He said he was very certain that he had not related anything but the facts and that he had committed many offenses against Our Lord after he began to serve Him but that he had never consented to mortal sin. His devotion, that is, his ease in finding God, had always continued to increase and now more than in his whole life. Each time and hour that he wanted to find God, he found Him. Now he also had visions very often, especially those mentioned above in which he saw Christ as the sun. This often happened while he was speaking of important matters, and it came to him as a confirmation.

He also had many visions when he said mass, and when he was drawing up the constitutions he had them with great frequency. He could now affirm this more easily because every day he wrote down what passed through his soul and he had it now in writing. He then showed me a fairly large bundle of writings and allowed me to read a good part of them.[7] Most were visions that he saw in confirmation of parts of the constitutions, at times seeing God the Father, at other times all three Persons of the Trinity, at other times Our Lady who interceded and at other times confirmed.

In particular he spoke to me about certain decisions over which

6. Ignatius is refering here to sections 169 through 189 of the *Spiritual Exercises* where he sets down rules for the proper choice of a way of life.

7. Only a portion of these writings, it appears, has survived. It consists of notes in diary form running from February 2, 1544 to February 27, 1545 and is known as the *Spiritual Journal* of St. Ignatius. The entries describe the visions, prayers and masses in connection with the drafting of the Constitutions which Câmara refers to in this final section of the autobiography. *MHSJ, Monumenta Ignatiana, Constitutiones* (Rome, 1934), I, 86–158, and *The Spiritual Journal of St. Ignatius Loyola*, trans. William J. Young, S. J. (Woodstock, Md., 1958).

he had said mass each day for forty days, each day with many tears. The question was whether the churches would have any income and whether the Society could make use of that.[8]

The habit which he observed while he was drafting the Constitutions was to say mass each day and to present the point that he was treating to God and to pray about it; he always said the prayer and the mass with tears.

I wanted to see all those papers relating to the constitutions, and I asked him to let me have them a while, but he did not want to.

8. The question concerned the degree of poverty the Society of Jesus would embrace, specifically whether the houses and churches of the Society should be permitted to have any fixed income. Ignatius decided not to allow a fixed income. The forty-day period during which Ignatius struggled with this question is the period covered in the first part of his *Spiritual Journal*—February 2 to March 12, 1544. On the stipulations regarding poverty in the Society, see *The Constitutions of the Society of Jesus*, trans. George E. Ganss, S.J. (St. Louis, 1970), pp. 251–59.

Appendixes

Ignatius's Letter to Isabel Roser
(December 19, 1538)

Ignatius wrote this letter to an old friend in Barcelona whom he had first met at the beginning of his pilgrimage in 1522–23.[1] She was a devoted admirer and had given Ignatius considerable support in the intervening years. The letter describes in some detail the initial difficulties Ignatius and his friends faced after they had arrived in Rome, as well as their early activities in the papal city; and in this regard it expands and supplements the last chapter of the autobiography. Needless to say, it casts great light on the beginnings of the Society of Jesus, the formal organization of which seems to be suggested in a passage toward the end of the letter.

May the grace and love of Christ our Lord be always to our favor and assistance.

I do believe that you are very anxious and, indeed, surprised because I have not written frequently to you, as I wished and desired; for if I should forget how much I owe Our Lord through your hands, with such sincere love and kindness, I think that His Divine Majesty would not be mindful of me, for you have always given so much for me out of love and reverence for Him. The reason, therefore, for my delay in writing has been because we were confident from day to day or from month to month of settling some business of ours so that we could inform you more certainly of our situation

1. The English translation has been made from the Spanish text in the *Monumenta Historica Societatis Jesu, Monumenta Ignatiana, Epistolae et Instructiones* (Madrid, 1903), I: 137–44.

98   *The Autobiography of St. Ignatius Loyola*

here. The business was such that for eight full months we have endured the most severe opposition or persecution that we have ever endured in this life. I do not mean that they have bothered our persons nor called us into court nor in any other way; but by spreading rumor among the people and by putting out unheard-of reports, they made us suspect and hateful to the people, causing great scandal so that we were forced to present ourselves before the legate and the governor of this city (for the pope had then gone to Nice), because of the great scandal caused among many people. We began to name and to summon some who had turned against us, so they might state before our superiors the evils they found in our life and teaching. And because in some way the affair is more easily understood from the beginning, I will give you some account of it.

It is more than a year since three of us belonging to the Society arrived here in Rome, as I remember having written to you. Two began at once to teach free of charge in the Sapienza College, the one, positive, and the other, scholastic theology, and this by command of the pope. I devoted myself entirely to giving and communicating the spiritual exercises to others, both in Rome and outside. We agreed on this so as to have some learned or distinguished men on our side or, better said, on the side of God our Lord, for His honor and glory, for ours is naught else but the praise and service of His Divine Majesty. We did this so that we would not encounter so much opposition among worldly people and thereafter might be able more freely to preach His most holy word, as we found the earth to be so barren of good fruit and abounding in bad. After we had gained some to our favor and opinion—persons of good education and estimation—by means of the exercises (through the help of God our Lord), at the end of four months from our arrival we decided to gather together all those of the Society in this city. When we were assembled, we strove diligently to obtain permission to preach, to exhort, and to hear confessions; the legate gave us a very full permission, even though in this matter many evil reports concerning us were given to his vicar to prevent the issuance of that permission.

After receiving it four or five of us began to preach on feast days and Sundays in various churches and to teach boys the commandments, the mortal sins, and so forth in other churches; all the while we continued the two classes in the Sapienza and also the confessions. All the others preached in the Italian tongue, but I alone in Spanish. There was a sufficiently large gathering of people for all the sermons, and, indeed, more than we thought would come, for three reasons. First, because the time was unusual; we began right after Easter when the other preachers for Lent and the principal feasts had ended. In this region it is the custom to preach only in Lent and Advent. Second, because commonly, after the austerities and sermons of

Lent are over, many on account of our sins are inclined afterward more to leisure and worldly pleasures than to other similar or new devotions. Third, because we do not believe that we are endowed with elegance or distinction, but for all that we do believe, because of many experiences, that Our Lord through His infinite and highest goodness does not forget us and through us, so lowly and of no account, helps and favors many others.

We then presented ourselves, and when two others were summoned and called, one of them found himself before the judges, quite the opposite of where he expected to be. The others whom we named to be summoned were so fearful that, not wishing nor daring to appear, they took steps against us so that we would have to proceed in the case before other judges. As they were persons, some with incomes of 1,000 ducats, some with 600, and others indeed of even greater importance, all of them courtiers and businessmen, they stirred up the cardinals and many other persons of importance in the curia so much that they made us spend a great deal of time in this conflict.

At last the most important among them, having been summoned, appeared before the legate and the governor and said that they had heard our sermons and lectures and so forth and found everything, both in our teaching and in our lives, in entire justification of us. With that the legate and the governor, who held us in very great esteem, wanted to leave the matter in silence, on account both of these persons and also of others. We often asked, as we thought it was just, that the evil or good there was in our teaching should be set forth in writing so that the scandal given to the people might be lifted; we were never able to obtain this, either out of justice or out of law. From this time on with the fear they had of justice, they no longer said against us the same things as before, at least not in public.

As we were unable to persuade them to give a sentence or declaration in our case, a friend of ours spoke to the pope after he returned from Nice, begging him to give a declaration in the case. Although the pope granted it, nothing happened, so two members of our Society also spoke to him. As he then left Rome for a castle in the suburbs [at Frascati], I went there and spoke to His Holiness alone in his room for an entire hour. Speaking to him there at length about our plans and intentions, I clearly related to him all the occasions when proceedings had been undertaken against me in Spain and in Paris, and also the times I had been imprisoned in Alcalá and Salamanca. I did this so that no one would be able to tell him more than what I told him and that he would be more inclined to make an inquiry concerning us and that in one way or another a sentence or declaration would be given about our teaching.

Finally, in order for us to teach and exhort it was very necessary to be held in good repute not only before God our Lord, but also before the people, and not to be suspect in our teaching and habits. I begged His Holiness, therefore, in the name of all of us, to provide a remedy, that is, that our teaching and habits should be investigated and examined by any ordinary judge whom His Holiness might appoint. For if they found evil, we wanted to be corrected and punished; if good, we wanted His Holiness to favor us. The pope, although he had reason for suspicion (with what I told him), took it very well, praising our abilities which we put to good use. Then, after he spoke to us for a while, exhorting us (indeed with the words of a true and righteous shepherd), he ordered the governor, who is a bishop and the chief justice of this city both in ecclesiastical and in secular affairs, to inquire immediately and diligently into our case. He carried out a new trial and did so with diligence, and the Pope on returning to Rome often spoke publicly in our favor and before our Society, for every two weeks the fathers are accustomed to go to hold a disputation during His Holiness's meal. Much of our storm has blown over and every day things get better so that in my judgment things are going very much as we would wish in the service and glory of God our Lord. We are now much sought out by some prelates and others who would like us, with the help of God our Lord, to bring forth good fruit in their lands. We remain here to await a greater opportunity.

Now it has pleased God our Lord that our case has been judged and settled. Concerning this something quite wonderful happened here; namely, that as it had been said of us and published here that we were fugitives from many countries, and especially from Paris, Spain, and Venice, at the very time that the sentence or declaration was given concerning us there were recently arrived here in Rome the regent Figueroa, who arrested me once in Alcalá and twice carried out proceedings against me, and the vicar-general of the legate to Venice, who also instituted proceedings against me (after we began to preach in the dominion of Venice), and Dr. Ory, who also instituted proceedings against me in Paris, and the bishop of Vicenza, where three or four of us preached for a short time; and all of them gave testimony about us. The cities of Siena, Bologna, and Ferrara also sent their authentic testimonies here, and the duke of Ferrara, besides sending testimony, took the affair very much to heart because of the dishonor done in our persons to God our Lord and wrote to his ambassador several times and to our Society, making the case his own, for he had seen the good fruit brought forth in his city and also in the other cities where we had labored (though we had not known quite how to sustain ourselves and to persevere there). For this we give thanks to God our Lord because from the time we began until the present moment we have never failed to give two or three sermons on every feast day and also two lectures every day; some were occupied with confessions and others with the spiritual exercises. Now that the sentence has been given, we hope to increase the sermons and also our classes for boys; and although the land may be sterile and barren, we cannot say in truth that we have lacked for things to do or that God our Lord has not effected more than our knowledge and understanding could achieve.

I do not expand upon the details, so as not to run on too much. In general God our Lord has made us very content. I will only say that there are four or five who are determined to enter our Society, and they have already persevered for many days and months in that determination. We do not dare to admit them as yet because this was one point among others charged against us, namely, that we received others and formed a congregation or religious community without apostolic authority. But now, although we are not united in our way of life, we are all united in spirit in order to proceed together in the future. We hope that God our Lord will soon dispose this in such a way that He may be better served and praised in all.

Since you have heard about our affairs and in what state they are, I ask you, for the love and reverence of God our Lord, to be very patient with me and to desire that He may wish to work through us whatever may be to His greater glory and praise; for, indeed, there are matters presently of great importance and weight. I will inform you more often of what is happening, and I tell you that undoubtedly if I forget you, I expect to be forgotten by my Creator and Lord. For this reason I am not so much concerned to discharge my duty or to give thanks in words, but you may be certain of this, that, besides the fact that all that you have done for me out of love and reverence for Him lives before God our Lord, you will share fully all the days of my life in all the things that His Divine Majesty may be pleased to work through me, making them worthy by His divine grace, just as you have always aided and so especially favored me in His divine service and praise. I ask to be very much remembered and commended to all the persons known to you and me, honest and devout in holy conversation and joined together in Christ our Lord.

I conclude, asking God our Lord through His infinite and supreme goodness to deign to give His grace fully to us so that we may know His most holy will and may fulfill it completely.

From Rome, December 19, 1538.

Poor in goodness,
Iñigo

While writing this, the Pope has ordered that provision be made through the governor that an order be given to the city to organize schools for boys, whom we might instruct in Christian doctrine, as we began to do previously. May it please God our Lord, since it is His affair, to deign to give us strength for His greater service and praise. I am sending the same declaration that was given here concerning us to Archdeacon Cazador (because it is in Latin), and he will communicate it to you.

A Letter to Diego de Gouvea
(November 23, 1538)

Diego de Gouvea was the principal of the college of Sainte-Barbe in Paris, the college which Ignatius, Peter Faber, Francis Xavier, and Simon Rodrigues had attended and from which they had received their master of arts. He was Portuguese, and, in addition to being an educator and theologian, he was frequently engaged in diplomatic tasks for the Portuguese king, John III.[1] On February 17, 1538, he had written to the king to suggest that he obtain the services of Ignatius and his companions (they had recently come to Rome) to help evangelize the Indies.[2] Later in the year Gouvea wrote to the companions themselves in Rome, urging them to go to the Indies. The letter published below is their response to Gouvea.[3] It was written by Peter Faber in the name of all his brothers, and it stresses that they have put themselves at the disposal of the pope and will do the work he assigns. Toward the end it gives expression to the view that a virtuous life iș the best defense of the faith, an interesting and rather Erasmian point of view to express to a Sorbonne theologian in the context of these times. Gouvea sent the letter he received from Faber and the others to the king of Portugal, who in August 1539

1. On Gouvea, see Luis de Matos, *Les Portugais à l'Université de Paris entre 1500 et 1550* (Coimbra, 1950), pp. 29ff and 125ff.
2. Marcel Bataillon, *Études sur le Portugal au temps de l'humanisme* (Coimbra, 1952), pp. 131–40, and Francisco Rodrigues, "O Dr. Gouveia e a entrada dos Jesuitas em Portugal," *Brotéria*, II (1926): 267–74.
3. The English translation has been made from the Latin text in the *Monumenta Historica Societatis Jesu, Monumenta Ignatiana, Epistolae et Instructiones* (Madrid, 1903), I:132–34.

instructed his ambassador at Rome, Pedro de Mascarenhas, to inquire about these men and their possible enlistment for missionary work. The upshot of the inquiries and negotiations that followed was that Francis Xavier and Simon Rodrigues left Rome for Lisbon in March 1540, the former to go on to India the following year, the latter to stay in Portugal and direct the establishment of a large Jesuit community there.

IHS

May the grace of our Lord Jesus Christ and peace be with all.

A few days ago your messenger arrived here with your letter to us. From him we heard the news concerning you, and from the letter we learned of your excellent recollection of us as well as of the great desire you have for the salvation of those souls in your Indies which are becoming white for the harvest. Would that we could satisfy you and moreover our own inclinations which are likewise zealous! But something at present stands in the way so that we cannot respond to the desires of many, to say nothing of yours. You will understand this from what I now explain. All of us who are mutually bound together in this Society have pledged ourselves to the supreme pontiff, seeing that he is the lord of the entire harvest of Christ. In this offering we have indicated to him that we are prepared for all that he may in Christ decide in our case. If, therefore, he should send us there where you summon us, we shall go rejoicing. The reason that we subjected ourselves in this way to his judgment and will was that we know that he has a greater knowledge of what is advantageous to the whole of Christendom.

There have not been lacking some who for a long time now have been trying to have us sent to those Indies which the Spaniards are daily acquiring for the emperor. A certain Spanish bishop and the envoy of the emperor had been especially persistent in this regard, but they learned that it is not the will of the supreme pontiff that we depart from here because even at Rome there is an abundant harvest. To be sure, the distance of places does not frighten us nor does the labor of learning the language. Let only that be done which above all is pleasing to Christ. Ask in our behalf, therefore, that He make us His ministers in the word of life. "There is no question of our being qualified in ourselves," rather our hope is in His abundance and riches.[4]

4. II Corinthians 3:5.

You will learn much about us and our affairs from the letter which we have written to our special friend and brother in Christ, Diego de Cáceres, a Spaniard.[5] He will show it to you. There you will see how many tribulations we have hitherto endured at Rome, and how we at last emerged unscathed. Even in Rome there are many to whom the light of the church's truth and life is hateful. Be you vigilant therefore, and with as much effort occupy yourself now in teaching the Christian people by the example of living as heretofore you exerted in defense of the faith and the church's teaching. For how do we believe the good God will preserve the truth of the holy faith in us, if we flee from virtue itself? It must be feared that the principal cause of errors of doctrine comes from errors of life, which unless they be corrected, the doctrinal errors will not be cleared from the way.

As we bring this letter to an end, it remains for us to beg you to deign to commend us to our most esteemed masters, Barthélemy, de Cornet, Piccard, Adam, Wancob, Laurency, Benoit, and all others, who gladly acknowledge being our teachers and us as their students and sons in Christ Jesus in whom farewell.

From the city of Rome, November 23, 1538

Yours in the Lord,

Peter Faber and his companions and brothers

---

5. Caceres was an early companion who later left the Society. He was at this time completing his studies in Paris.

The First Sketch of the Institute of the Society of Jesus (1539)

In the spring of 1539 Ignatius and his companions in Rome engaged in long discussions about organizing more formally as a religious order, and, having agreed to do so, they debated the character and aims of their proposed association. The decisions they reached were summarized in a brief statement of five articles for submission to the pope for his approval. This statement, the original sketch or *prima summa* of the Society of Jesus, is the earliest declaration concerning the new order.[1] It was submitted probably at the end of June, carefully examined by Tommaso Badia, the papal theologian, and approved by Paul III on September 3. Cardinal Gasparo Contarini, the leader of the reform party at Rome, served as intermediary for the nascent Society in obtaining papal approval. The statement was substantially reproduced in the official bull of institution, *Regimini militantis ecclesiae,* issued in September 1540.[2]

1. Whoever wishes to be a soldier of God under the standard of the cross and serve the Lord alone and His vicar on earth in our Society, which we desire to be designated by the name of Jesus, should, after a solemn vow of perpetual chastity, bear in mind that he is part of a community founded principally for the advancement of souls in Christian life and doctrine and for the propagation of the faith by the ministry of the word, by spiritual

1. The English translation has been made from the Latin text in the *Monumenta Historica Societatis Jesu, Monumenta Ignatiana, Constitutiones* (Rome, 1934), I: 16–20.
2. This bull may be found in John C. Olin, *The Catholic Reformation: Savonarola to Ignatius Loyola* (New York, 1969), pp. 203–08.

exercises, by works of charity, and expressly by the instruction in Christianity of children and the uneducated. He should especially direct himself and take care to have always before his eyes first God, then the plan of this his Institute, which is, as it were, a way to Him, and to strive with all his strength to attain this goal which God has set before him, each one, however, according to the grace given him by the Holy Spirit and the particular grade of his vocation, lest anyone by chance yield to zeal but not with knowledge. The decision about the particular grade of each one and the entire selection and distribution of duties shall be in the hands of the *prepositus* or prelate chosen by us so that the appropriate order necessary in every well-organized community may be preserved. This *prepositus* with the advice of the brothers shall have the authority to establish in council constitutions profitable for the achievement of this goal set before us, a majority of the votes always having the right to decide. In matters that are more serious and lasting, a council should be understood to be the greater part of the whole Society which can conveniently be summoned by the *prepositus;* in lighter and more temporary matters it will be all those who happen to be present in the place where our *prepositus* resides. All right to execute and command, however, will be in the power of the *prepositus.*

2. All the companions should know and daily bear in mind, not only when they first make their profession but as long as they live, that this entire Society and each one individually are soldiers of God under faithful obedience to our most holy lord Paul III and his successors and are thus under the command of the vicar of Christ and his divine power not only as having the obligation to him which is common to all clerics, but also as being so bound by the bond of a vow that whatever His Holiness commands pertaining to the advancement of souls and the propagation of the faith we must immediately carry out, without any evasion or excuse, as far as in us lies, whether he sends us to the Turks or to the New World or to the Lutherans or to others be they infidel or faithful. For this reason those who would join us, and before they put their shoulders to this burden, should meditate long and hard whether they possess the spiritual riches to enable them to complete this tower in keeping with the counsel of the Lord, that is, whether the Holy Spirit who incites them promises them sufficient grace so that with His help they may hope to bear the weight of this vocation. And after, with the Lord inspiring them, they have enlisted in this militia of Jesus Christ, they must have their loins girded day and night and be ready to discharge so great a debt. Lest, however, there could be among us any ambition for or rejection of particular missions or assignments, let each one promise never to take the matter of such missions up with the pontiff either directly or indirectly, but to leave all this care to God and to His vicar and to the

prepositus of the Society. The *prepositus,* like the others, shall also promise to take nothing up with the pontiff either one way or another concerning a mission of his own, except with the advice of the Society.

3. Each one shall vow that he will be obedient to the *prepositus* of the Society in all things relevant to the observance of this our rule. The latter, moreover, shall ordain what he deems to be appropriate for achieving the goal set before him by God and the Society. In his office, however, let him always remember the kindness, gentleness, and charity of Christ and the pattern of Peter and Paul, and let both him and the council constantly keep this norm in view. Particularly let them hold esteemed the instruction of children and the uneducated in the Christian doctrine of the Ten Commandments and other similar rudiments, whatever will seem suitable to them in accordance with the circumstances of persons, places, and times. For it is very necessary that the *prepositus* and the council give this matter the most diligent attention since among our neighbors the edifice of faith cannot arise without a foundation and since among us there is the danger that, as anyone becomes more learned, he may attempt to decline this assignment as being at first glance less splendid, although in reality there is none more faithful either for the edification of neighbors or for the practice of the duties of charity and humility in our own case. The subjects, that is, the members of the Society, both for the great utility of the order and for the sake of the continual practice of humility which has never been sufficiently praised, shall be always bound to obey the *prepositus* in all things pertaining to the Institute of the Society, and they shall acknowledge and venerate as far as it is fitting Christ as though present in him.

4. Since we have learned from experience that a life as far removed as possible from every taint of avarice and as close as possible to evangelical poverty is more joyful, more pure, and more appropriate for the edification of neighbor and since we know that our Lord Jesus Christ will provide what is necessary for food and clothing for His servants seeking only the Kingdom of God, each and all shall vow perpetual poverty, declaring that they cannot either individually or in common acquire any civil right to any real property or any revenue or income for the maintenance and use of the Society. Rather let them be content to delight in the use only of the necessary things, with the owners permitting, and to receive money and the value of things given them in order to provide the necessities for themselves. They shall be able, however, to acquire the civil right to real property and to income in order to bring together some talented students and instruct them especially in sacred letters at the universities, that is, for the support of those students who desire to advance in the spirit and in letters and at length to be received in our Society after probation when the period of their studies has been finished.

5. All the companions who are in holy orders, even though they can acquire no right to benefices and incomes, shall be bound to say the office according to the rites of the church, but not in choir lest they be led away from the works of charity to which we have all dedicated ourselves. For this reason neither organs nor singing shall be used in their masses and religious ceremonies, for these, which laudably adorn the divine worship of the other clerics and religious and have been found to arouse and move souls by virtue of their hymns and rites, we have found to be a considerable hindrance to us, since as a consequence of the nature of our vocation, besides other necessary duties, we must frequently be occupied a great part of the day and even of the night in comforting the sick both in body and in spirit.

These are the features concerning our profession which we are able to explain in a kind of sketch, and we do this now in order to instruct in a brief account both those who question us about our plan of life and also our posterity, if, God willing, we shall ever have imitators of this way. And since we have learned that this way has many and great difficulties connected with it, we have thought it useful to admonish those not to infringe, under the pretext of what is right, upon these two prohibitions. One is that they do not impose on the companions under pain of mortal sin any fasts, disciplines, baring of feet or head, style of dress, type of food, penances, hair shirts, and other torments of the flesh. These, however, we do not therefore prohibit because we condemn them, for we greatly praise and honor them in the men who observe them, but only because we do not wish ours to be crushed by so many burdens at the same time joined together or to allege any excuse for not carrying out what we have set before ourselves. Everyone can, however, exercise himself faithfully in those practises he deems to be necessary and useful for himself, as long as the *prepositus* does not prohibit them. The other is that no one be received into the Society unless he first has been tested for a long time and most diligently. And when he appears prudent in Christ and distinguished [*conspicuus*] both in learning and in holiness of life, then at length let him be admitted to the militia of Jesus Christ, who may deign to favor our feeble undertakings for the glory of God the Father, to whom alone be glory and honor forever. Amen.

Bibliographical Note

The bibliography relevant to Ignatius Loyola and the early Jesuits is very extensive. There are fortunately some excellent and up-to-date bibliographical guides for anyone digging deeply into this subject:

Jean-François Gilmont, S.J., and Paul Daman, S.J., *Bibliographie ignatienne* *(1894–1957)* (Paris-Louvain, 1958)

Jean-François Gilmont, S.J., *Les écrits spirituels des premiers Jésuites* (Rome, 1961)

I. Iparraguirre, S.J., *Oriéntaciones bibliograficas sobre San Ignacio de Loyola* 2d ed. (Rome, 1965)

Laszlo Polgar, S.J., *Bibliography of the History of the Society of Jesus* (Rome, 1967).

The great source collection on Ignatius and the first Jesuits is the *Monumenta Historica Societatis Jesu,* 100 volumes (Madrid-Rome, 1894–1969), an important subdivision of which is entitled the *Monumenta Ignatiana.* The latter contains the writings, correspondence, early *vitae,* and so forth of St. Ignatius and is divided into four series consisting of (1) the correspondence, (2) the spiritual exercises, (3) the constitutions of the Society of Jesus, and (4) early writings about Ignatius. The fourth series has been replaced by the *Fontes narrativi de S. Ignacio de Loyola,* 4 vols (Rome, 1943–65), and it is from the critical text in Volume 1 of this set that we have made our translation of the autobiography. The second series has also been replaced by a new critical edition of the spiritual exercises, Volume 100 of the *MHSJ* (Rome, 1969).

There are several translations into English of the spiritual exercises, the best being that of Louis J. Puhl, S.J. (Westminister, Md., 1951, 2d ed., Chicago, n.d.). The constitutions of the Society of Jesus have been translated with an introduction and commentary by George E. Ganss, S.J. (St. Louis, 1970). There are two editions in English of selected letters of Ignatius: Hugo Rahner, S.J., *Saint Ignatius Loyola, Letters to Women* (New York, 1960), and *Letters of St. Ignatius of Loyola,* trans. William J. Young, S.J. (Chicago, 1959).

Works about Ignatius and the Society of Jesus are legion, though there is no definitive or completely satisfactory book on the saint and the establishment of the new order. The best biography, perhaps, is Paul Dudon, S.J., *St. Ignatius of Loyola,* trans. William J. Young, S.J. (Milwaukee, 1949). Paul Van Dyke, *Ignatius Loyola, the Founder of the Jesuits* (New York, 1926) is a fairly standard American biography. The best-known and most readily available works on the subject are those of James Brodrick, S.J.: *The Origin of the Jesuits* (New York, 1940, paperback ed., New York, 1960); and *Saint Ignatius Loyola, the Pilgrim Years, 1491–1538* (New York, 1956). An excellent account of Ignatius's early years and background is Pedro Leturia, S.J., *Iñigo de Loyola,* trans. Aloysius J. Owen, S.J. (Syracuse, 1949). A superb book of photographs with text on the life of the saint is Leonard von Matt and Hugo Rahner, S.J., *St. Ignatius of Loyola, a Pictorial Biography,* trans. John Murray, S.J. (Chicago, 1956).

On the thought and spirituality of Ignatius the basic work is Joseph de Guibert, S.J., *The Jesuits, Their Spiritual Doctrine and Practice,* trans. William J. Young, S.J. (Chicago, 1964). Hugo Rahner, S.J., *The Spirituality of St. Ignatius Loyola,* trans. F. J. Smith, S.J. (Westminister, Md., 1953); and Rahner, *Ignatius the Theologian,* trans. Michael Barry (New York, 1968), are also important studies. Last but far from least, H. O. Evennett, *The Spirit of the Counter-Reformation,* ed. John Bossy (Cambridge, 1968), especially chaps. 3 and 4, affords an excellent historical introduction to Ignatius and the new Society.

Several recent titles should be appended to this Bibliographical Note. Foremost are two new but very different biographies of Ignatius: Philip Caraman, S.J., *Ignatius Loyola, a Biography of the Founder of the Jesuits* (San Francisco, 1990), and W. W. Meissner, S.J., *Ignatius of Loyola, the Psychology of a Saint* (New Haven, 1992). Two shorter studies pose and discuss some key questions concerning Ignatius: Philip Endean, S.J., "Who Do You Say Ignatius Is? Jesuit Fundamentalism and Beyond," *Studies in the Spirituality of Jesuits,* 19/5 (November 1987), and John W.

O'Malley, S.J., "Was Ignatius Loyola a Church Reformer? How to Look at Early Modern Catholicism," *The Catholic Historical Review* LXXVII, No. 2 (April 1991), 177–93. Especially relevant to the *Autobiography* are two earlier studies: Javier Osuna, S.J., *Friends in the Lord*, trans. Nicholas King, S.J. (London, 1974), and John C. Olin, "The Idea of Pilgrimage in the Experience of Ignatius Loyola," *Church History* 48, No. 4 (December 1979), 387–97, and reprinted in John C. Olin, *Catholic Reform from Cardinal Ximenes to the Council of Trent* (New York, 1990), pp. 129–42. Finally, Father O'Malley's broadly based article "Renaissance Humanism and the Religious Culture of the First Jesuits," *Heythrop Journal* XXXI (October 1990), 471–87, should be noted for the important contextual thesis it presents.